Advance Praise for A Life in Print

"A Life in Print is a refreshingly honest expression of a life's work by a journalist who went to Washington but never lost touch with the land or the values of family and of the people he and his newspapers served. Jim Gannon's love of language and affection for his Irish heritage and Iowa roots shine through this wonderful collection."

Robert Giles, Curator
The Nieman Foundation at Harvard University

"Some columns yellow like the newspaper on which they originally appeared. The selections from the sterling career of newsman Jim Gannon are a happy exception. He writes with clarity and wit not so much about yesterday's headlines as about universal themes that resonate through the years: family and roots and the timeless promise of land. You will like these crystalline vignettes of an American life. And you will like even more the man who lived them."

Carol Stevens, Managing Editor/News
USA TODAY

"The columns constitute a kind of autobiographical journey through a life in newspaper work. They are written with passion and grace."

Arnold Garson, Publisher
Sioux Falls (SD) Argus Leader

"It is wonderful…With each page you'll repeat yourself: I wish I'd written that."

David Shribman, Executive Editor
Pittsburgh Post-Gazette

Advance Praise for A Life in Print

"A Life in Print comes alive in the warm, insightful and touching prose that Jim Gannon has offered to readers over the years. Jim's writings consistently pull together the strands of our lives-the personal pains and joys, the economy of which we're all a part, and the sometimes seemingly distant world of public policy-in ways that make compelling reading. Thanks perhaps to Jim's inherent Irish optimism and fundamental religious faith, his columns put life in perspective in a dinner-table fashion that's understandable and often even comforting."

Byron Calame, former deputy managing editor,
The Wall Street Journal

"It's a great book!"

Congressman John D. Dingell of Michigan

"From poignant glimpses of a family stricken by tragedy, to white-knuckle moments on the nation's stage, A Life in Print allows the reader to see the world through the prism of a remarkable journalist, who masterfully comments on 'the stuff of life'."

John Siniff, Executive Forum Editor,
USA Today

A LIFE IN PRINT

Selections from the work of a
reporter, columnist and editor

By James P. Gannon

*From the pages of The Wall Street Journal,
The Des Moines Register and The Detroit News*

Blackwater Publications
2005

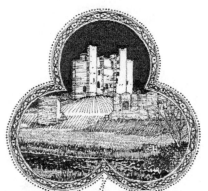

Blackwater Publications

A LIFE IN PRINT:

Selections from the work of a reporter, columnist and editor

The author wishes to thank The Wall Street Journal, The Des Moines Register and The Detroit News for permission to reprint articles contained herein.

ISBN 0-976452804
Library of Congress Catalog Number: 2005900100

Published by Blackwater Publications
P.O. Box 80
Boston, VA 22713
www.blackwaterpublications.com
e-mail: blackwaterpub@earthlink.net

Cover Design and book typography by Michele Snider
designmws@aol.com or (540) 829-5281

Logo by Thomas Tepper: Trim Castle, County Meath, Ireland

*To Joan, my guiding light,
and to our children who light up our lives.*

TABLE OF CONTENTS

INTRODUCTION

One of the journalistic heroes of my youth, James Reston of The New York Times, wrote in the introduction to a collection of his own writings that "a newspaper column, like a fish, should be consumed when fresh; otherwise it is not only indigestible but unspeakable." He added: "Nothing cuts a man down to proper size quicker than prowling through the graveyard of old clippings for a few signs of life."

Lately I have been prowling through my own graveyard of newspaper clippings, produced over a 33-year career in daily journalism, looking for those rare signs of life. It is a humbling business. What seemed so compelling and clever at the time it went to press can be exposed, in the revealing light of history, as simply the wrong-headed conventional wisdom of the times, or worse.

Most of what a newspaper reporter or columnist writes is, and should be, quickly forgotten. Only occasionally will even a gifted writer have something to say that holds up to scrutiny years later. In my own case, I have tried to select for this collection a variety of pieces that seem worth preserving in a form more enduring than yellowing and brittle newspaper clippings.

The columns and articles chosen for this book are not entirely representative of the work I did as a reporter and columnist over a third of a century of newspapering. The first 17 years of my career were spent as a reporter for The Wall Street Journal, in Chicago, Pittsburgh, and Washington, DC. As such, I focused on the daily flow of news — in business, the economy, government and politics — all of which is the stuff of yesterday's headlines. Little of this remains relevant or enlightening years later. Thus, there are relatively few pieces in this collection from my Wall Street Journal work, even though I consider that work among the best I ever produced.

After I moved to Iowa in 1978 — first as Executive Editor of The Des Moines Register and Tribune, and later as Editor — I began writing a regular weekly column for the Sunday Register. This gave me freedom to go beyond the day's news and write on any subject of my choosing, from a more personal viewpoint. While most of my columns dealt with events in the news, I also wrote about more personal things — everything from my love of trains and country music to my appreciation of my Irish roots and memories of my father.

After ten years in Des Moines, I returned to Washington as Bureau Chief of The Detroit News and a national affairs columnist for the Gannett Co. newspapers. My weekly column of commentary during the six years I spent in that job generally centered on politics, government and world events. But, as in Des Moines, I had freedom to write on the ordinary stuff of everyday life — a son's graduation from college, the tragic death of a Vietnam veteran in the family, or my teenage children's near-fatal auto accident.

As a writer, I found that it was these personal, human topics that connected with the reader most intensely. Columns on politics, the economy, the latest outrage in Washington, or ominous threats of war might elicit little or no response, while a personal piece about your daughter's wedding or your Iowa farm would provoke many letters and much comment. It was the universal stuff of human experience — life and death, joy and heartbreak — that connected with people. And it is such columns that seem to have some enduring value many years after their first publication.

Thus, in picking pieces for this collection, I found those personal columns seemed most worthy of reprinting. I have included a number of pieces on politics, presidents, wars and world events. But an even larger number of columns deal with life as we lived it and newspaper work as we experienced it. Much of what I wrote is best forgotten, but these "signs of life" from my clippings graveyard represent something I think worth preserving — ideas, values, memories, victories and defeats — that make up the stuff of life. They are, in the end, the things that matter.

Finally, I would like to express thanks to the newspapers for their permission to reprint these pieces. Most of all, I want to thank my wife Joan and my children for all the years of support and understanding through 33 years of living with a newspaper man — for all the evenings I got home too late for supper, for the weeks away on some political campaign or foreign assignment, for all the school plays and teacher meetings I missed, for the moving from city to city in pursuit of career. They lived my newspaper years with me, and while I reaped the glory and honors, they helped carry the burden. They matter much more to me than anything I ever wrote.

James P. Gannon
June 25, 2004

1

FAMILY

"All this changed him, as it changed a generation of Americans. The bottom of their world fell out, and nobody could convince them later that it wouldn't happen again, even in the fat years of prosperity that followed. For more than 40 years, he lived convinced that another depression was coming, and he ordered his life and that of his family accordingly."

ON FATHER'S DAY, THE REMEMBRANCE OF ORDINARY THINGS

Des Moines Sunday Register, June 15, 1980

He was tall and thin, and had straight, white hair which he slicked back with Vaseline hair oil that left a permanent greasy spot on the upholstery of the high-backed chair where he seemed to live, reading his newspapers.

When I was small and didn't want to go upstairs alone to bed, I would drag out my pillow and lie down beside his chair, and fall asleep while he puffed his Chesterfields and silently devoured the news. I don't remember him carrying me up to bed, though he certainly did so many times.

We didn't play ball together or go fishing or pal around. He was always giving me quarters to go to the movies, or sometimes a dollar for no reason at all, and I would say, "Dad, I don't need this," and he would just say "Take it" and I would take it.

> **We didn't play ball together or go fishing or pal around. He was always giving me quarters to go to the movies.**

When he wasn't in his chair reading his newspapers, he usually was gone, at work in a Minneapolis office, doing things I didn't understand, or else traveling by train to the Dakotas, going from one small town to another, drumming up business for his grain firm at dingy country elevators. There were a few times, in the summers of my adolescence, when I accompanied him, and I recall sitting in those dusty offices of small-town elevators, wondering how anyone could stand making a living in such drudgery.

We didn't take vacations, but we had a modest cottage near Lake

Minnetonka where we spent much of the summer. He would drive out there after work in his 1940 Chevrolet, or later, his 1948 Dodge, and spend the night, before driving back into the city for another day at the office. Sometimes he would cut the grass, but mostly he just brought his newspapers and sat on a rocker on the porch, where I would play in a hammock that smelled musty from being in a closed-up cottage all winter. The hammock was strung up on the screened porch because the mosquitoes were so thick outside that you couldn't go out in the evening.

There wasn't much conversation. It was mostly about baseball or the weather. There was a 50-year gap between us, and that is hard to bridge when one is 10 and the other 60. But the gap seemed much narrower later, when I was 25 and he was 75 and we could talk of adult things.

The gap narrowed steadily in those last few years, and as we both grew older and I gained some perspective on his life, there wasn't much of a gap at all. He never knew his father, who had died in 1890, the year after he was born, so he was coming at this father-son relationship with no experience, either good or bad. When I think that my grandfather died in the previous century, nearly 50 years before I was born, I get an odd, disconnected feeling, as if one whole generation in my family had been mysteriously skipped. Some people my age still have living grandfathers, but my father's father never saw the 20th century.

"I never knew my father," he would say, but that's about all he could say on the subject. How that affected him, I suppose I'll never know. But every time Father's Day rolls around, and I think of him, I am thankful for a rich store of mundane memories, the remembrance of ordinary things, like the pillow by his chair, the quiet of a screened porch, and a quarter to go to the movies.

Mugged by the Depression

The Des Moines Sunday Register, February 27, 1983

For most of his life, my father lived in a psychological shadow cast by the economic catastrophe of his lifetime, the Great Depression of the 1930s.

He was a rising young businessman in Minneapolis in 1929 when the stock market crashed and ushered in a decade that impoverished and baffled him, striking blows against both his physical health and his confidence. Never before a sickly man, he developed asthma in the 1930s and probably had doubts about surviving the Depression, as he watched his business and his modest personal wealth wither in the Depression's economic drought, just as the crops withered in the dusty failure years.

He survived it, and he later prospered, but he was not unmarked. For the rest of his ample life — all through the prosperous '50s, '60s and into the early '70s — he waited for it to happen again. He was convinced that another economic crash would come, despite the strong tide of prosperity that the country rode in those years. Like a man who has been mugged, he walked through the rest of his life glancing over his shoulder, seeing dark visions in the shadows, one hand clasped firmly on his wallet.

The Depression changed his thinking about money, about life. Having lost everything once, he worked feverishly to restore his family's financial security when given a second chance. He feared debt and hated borrowing. He became a fierce disciple of saving and a stern critic of any non-essential spending.

He lived modestly, and though he was extraordinarily generous to his children, he was miserly when it came to himself. He was a Cadillac of a man, but he insisted on driving Chevrolets. He was sure, in the midst of the country's most prosperous era, that the politicians would ruin everything with foolish spending, inflation and debt, and thus bring on another economic debacle.

He was right, of course.

He died in 1973, just as everything started coming unstuck. He didn't live to see the oil sheiks drive up the price of petroleum tenfold (he thought gasoline was high at 33 cents a

He bought some South Dakota rangeland at $10 an acre and was tickled pink to sell at $40.

gallon) and he didn't live to see the bankers put the prime rate at 20 percent (he was outraged at the thought of a 7-percent mortgage) and he would not have believed farmland at $2,500 an acre (he bought some South Dakota range-land at $10 an acre and was tickled pink to sell at $40). He thought a budget deficit was a sin, and he never could have imagined that a President Reagan — Ronald Reagan, the guy he thought was the Great White Hope of the hard-money types! — would be proposing deficits of maybe $200 billion.

He was spared living through what he feared — a decade of roaring inflation that brought on, as he knew it would, an economic bust of high unemployment, business bankruptcies and farmers' distress. He was as prescient as I was blind, and he would have called all that we have lived through an entirely predictable depression.

And now they say it's ending, and maybe they are right. There are solid signs of life in the latest economic indicators, and the smart-money boys on Wall Street are betting millions that we've survived it all. The U.S. economy appears ready to rebound as lower inflation, lower interest rates and lower oil prices provide some stimulus, just as their opposites provided depressants. But how will we all emerge from this, psychologically?

That's the question that my father's example raises now. For we as a nation emerge twice-scarred from the economic turmoil of the past decade. After getting hooked on the inflation drug, can we go cold-turkey into a non-inflationary climate and adjust to it?

How do we psychologically adjust to falling farmland prices, falling home prices, declining wage and salary gains? Now the game has changed, and the new rules of play require a new mind-set. Borrowing more to buy more to cash in on inflation doesn't work now; you'd better plan to live in that house you've got, because you're not going to be able to automatically cash it in on a bigger one, thanks to inflation. You can't plan on a big inflation-driven pay increase any more, either, as millions of workers are discovering. It's time to lower expectations — if we can.

The inflation scar is only half of the psychological adjustment we face. For the many who have lost jobs, lost businesses, lost farms and lost faith in the future, there is the question my father faced: Will there be a second chance? This depression — let's not kid ourselves about what to call it — has severely shaken the confidence of millions of working men and women, investors, business executives, farmers, bankers. It will take time to repair that psychological damage.

There is now a new generation of Americans who have been mugged by the economy. If today's people have the guts and the drive of those who survived the Great Depression, they will survive — perhaps even prosper. But they will not walk away from this unmarked. They will go through life waiting for it to happen again.

Sorry, Dad, I didn't understand before. Now I do.

A TALE OF THREE GENERATIONS

The Des Moines Sunday Register, October 28, 1979

All the recent stories replaying the great stock market crash of 1929 have prompted memories and some musings. What happened fifty years ago was before my time, but it shaped the early part of my life, and I suspect that what is happening now in the American economy will shape the lives of my children and their generation.

Pardon me for getting personal, but the best way to explain what I have to say is to do it in terms of three very different generations: my father's, mine and my children's. I think this three-generations theory explains a lot about the way people used to be, the way they are now, and what they're likely to become in the future.

I didn't experience 1929, but my father did. He was 40 years old then (as I am now), and he was just beginning to "make it" in the business world. He had a new Auburn automobile, thick, black hair, confidence and a bunch of high-flying stocks. By the mid-thirties, he had an old car, white hair, worries and asthma. He was a grain merchant in Minneapolis, and he watched as the market crash was followed by the Great Depression, crop failures, bank foreclosures and a plague of grasshoppers.

I remember him telling of the grasshoppers. He was traveling the Dakotas in those days, driving from country elevator to country elevator, a desperate man trying to drum up business from other desperate men. The grasshoppers were so thick, he said, that the blacktop highway would be covered with them, and the car would slide and slither as it crushed the carpet of bugs. The dust would blow across those desolate prairies; where crops were being eaten alive on farms that were being taken over by the banks, and he would ride along in solitary confinement with his thoughts. He never gave up in despair, though I am not sure why.

All this changed him, as it changed a generation of Americans. The bottom of their world fell out, and nobody could convince them later that it wouldn't happen again, even in the fat years of prosperity that followed. For more than 40 years, he lived convinced that another depression was coming, and he ordered his life and that of his family accordingly. He saved money, shunned debt, counseled frugality and lived far below his means. He had a Chevrolet mentality even after fighting his way back into a Cadillac class of businessmen.

That is not the way of my generation. I grew up on prosperity. Everything got bigger and better, year after year. The postwar boom years brought suburban developments, gas-guzzling cars with fins, college for everybody, the certainty of a job, color TV, jet travel and wine with dinner. (We had wine once a year, when I was growing up — on Thanksgiving.) There were no limits to what the economy could do for 25 years after the end of World War II. Onward and upward, there's more where that came from: Those were the attitudes that shaped this first postwar generation.

And now the second postwar generation is growing up in a wholly new atmosphere. Unstoppable inflation and scarcity of key resources, notably oil, are the new attitude-shaping forces that are at work on my children, just as depression was my father's touchstone and prosperity has been mine.

As things go now, they are inheriting a world where prices double every seven years. We've built for them an economy intended to run on cheap oil, when there is no more cheap oil: big houses full of energy-gobbling gadgets, double-garages full of cars, snowmobiles and minibikes, back yards cluttered with speedboats, Winnebagos, heated pools and gas grills. What will they do with that world? Dismantle it?

We of the Prosperity Generation grew confident and became an ambitious people who could do it all and have it all and still want more.

I think I detect a new anxiety among the Inflation Generation, the children of the Prosperity Generation. If a good house costs nearly $100,000 now, what will it cost in another 10 years? If college costs $5,000 or more a year now, what will it cost in another few years? If gasoline has jumped from 65 cents to $1 a gallon in the past year, what is to prevent it from going to $2 a gallon this year and $4 a gallon the next? Gee, dad, I'll never have a Winnebago.

Americans of the Depression Generation grew cautious and became a conservative people who were thankful for small blessings, like having enough to eat. We of the Prosperity Generation grew confident and became an ambitious people who could do it all and have it all and still want more. And what of our children of the Inflation Generation? The ones nearing maturity now are growing anxious and are becoming an uncertain people facing economic limits that didn't exist for the generation before them.

Sometimes I think it is the Prosperity Generation that is the aberration — a class of people growing up on an unreal boom sandwiched in between the hard times before and the hard times ahead. But I suppose that only marks me as my father's son, touched by that nagging worry that hard times are sure to return. On the 50th anniversary of the Great Crash, it is easy to get carried away with visions of another one. It's easy — and silly.

Well, *probably* silly.

SO YOU ARE OFF TO COLLEGE — IT WAS EASIER FOR YOUR DAD

The Des Moines Sunday Register, August 24, 1980

Dear Julie:

So you are going off to college. I did that once myself, and I survived the experience, so I am not worried about you. But there are a few times in life when a father thinks he is expected to give wise counsel to his offspring, and this is one of those occasions, so bear with me while I pay the dues of parenthood.

I remember my college days as if they were yesterday, though my experience is probably irrelevant to the 1980s. I went to college toward the end of the Medieval Era, when Eisenhower was president. Society was different then. There were rules. The rules at my college sound hilarious today. The dorms were segregated — some all men, some all women. The only woman a guy could have in his room was his mother — once a year. You had to be in at 11 p.m. on weeknights and 1 a.m. on weekends. You couldn't have beer or liquor in your room and the only thing anybody even thought of smoking was tobacco.

> You also will encounter a professor with an identity problem — one who confuses himself with God.

No, I am not putting you on. That's the way it really was. We hated the rules, of course, and ridiculed them, but they provided a security network that kept us from having to decide whether to stay out all night, or keep a bottle or a bedmate in our rooms. All this made it easier to concentrate on Botany and Latin (yes, I know, it is entirely fitting that we actually studied an ancient, dead language).

College will be different for you. You'll come and go as you please, keep your own hours, set your own style, strike your own balance between work and pleasure, and decide what will constitute the latter. That's OK — you are an adult now and can plunge right in to adult decision-making, but I can't help thinking I was lucky in being able to postpone that for a while.

You'll meet all kinds of people. Not all of them will share your values. Some of them will have a radically different way of looking at life, and for the first time, you'll have a chance to compare what you believe with beliefs of others that challenge your own. This process is called education, and what it yields, ideally, is maturity. Don't be afraid of it. You'll never know whether you really believe all the things you think you believe until you hear some intelligent, articulate person rip your beliefs apart and hand you the pieces — to see if you can put them back together.

If you are lucky, you will encounter one or two personalities of towering stature and influence, who will enlarge your own horizons. I remember two at Marquette: a fugitive from the Irish Republican Army named Thomas Patrick Whelan, who made the writings of Shakespeare come alive for a generation of unlettered Midwestern sophomores, including me; and a giant of journalism education named Jeremiah L. O'Sulllvan, a man of great heart and understanding, who told his classes of would-be hard-nosed reporters that they should "write with compassion for your fellow human beings."

Unless human nature has changed, you also will encounter a professor with an identity problem — one who confuses himself with God. He is to be humored, and then avoided in signing up for the next semester's courses. He is not as dangerous, however, as the professor with the other identity problem — the one who thinks he's a peer and pal of the students, just a regular guy who wants to be "relevant" and "interactive." He is to be avoided like a three-dollar bill.

Among your fellow students, you will meet some very weird individuals; I particularly remember one young fellow from Boston who ate nothing but peanut-butter sandwiches for a full semester, and then dropped out, malnourished; and another from New Jersey who stayed up all night and slept all day — except for times when he went from room to room stealing from students who went to class.

More important, however, you will meet people you like and you will make a few good friends that will last a lifetime. You cannot share four years of close, stimulating experiences — discovering new ideas, discussing your dreams until dawn, comforting a disturbed, failing fellow student — without learning much about them and about yourself. You'll find people you can rely on, and others who will need to rely on you, and you'll come away from it all sharing a bond that will wear very well through the years.

You'll learn new facts and new ideas, but if the process works the way it should, the most important thing you'll learn is to love learning. You'll acquire an appetite for books — books that you don't have to read — and an ability to discriminate between scholarship and sophistry.

What this all amounts to is a test of all you are and all you can possibly be — a challenge to the mind, the heart, and the will — that inevitably reshapes and refines those who rise to it. College is a mountain daring to be climbed, and the atmosphere at the peak is rarefied and somewhat out-of-this-world, sometimes prompting giddiness but also a clarity of vision that brings to view horizons yet unseen. You should come down from the mountaintop with a much better grasp of the shape of the world around you and the direction of the road that lies ahead.

I know you are anxious to get on with it, and to do well so that you can embark on a career in the "real world." But do not think too far ahead. The future will arrive soon enough, and for now you are best advised to wring everything you can from old professors and quiet walks on campus, essays on history and midnight discussions, football games and pub-crawling.

Take it from a nostalgic, middle-aged man who has climbed that mountain: You'll probably not find another as fulfilling or as fun.

Lovingly,

Your Father

–P.S. Now that you are leaving, can I have my car back?

LETTER TO A NEW GRADUATE

The Des Moines Sunday Register, June 3, 1984

Dear Julie: It hardly seems possible that it is nearly four years since I wrote that letter to you as you departed for college. Now you are graduating, and I again feel an urge to say something fatherly.

It's harder now to know just what to say. When you departed for college, I felt that I knew the environment you'd enter, the opportunities you'd face, and the pitfalls you should avoid. Even though nearly a quarter-century had passed since my college days, and even though the old mores had given way to the new freedom, life on campus for you was not going to be radically different, I believed. You were nervous and insecure, like all freshmen, and I was confident in you, like all fathers. And I was right, wasn't I?

Now you are confident and proud, as you should be. You proved not only that you could compete on an academic fast-track, but also that you could excel. You're no longer intimidated by Eastern prep-school types, and no longer afraid to challenge a silly idea just because it's advanced by an important person. That new self-confidence will serve you well.

But isn't it odd? Now I am the one who is nervous and insecure. Not about you, I hasten to add, but about the world we have prepared for you and your generation. We have educated you to be the best and brightest hope of the nation, brimming with idealism. But we are inviting you into a world so radically out of line with those high-minded things that what you have become may seem not what you need to be to get along on the low road of reality.

In college, you have learned to value learning; in the world, you will find that we place a higher value on the work of athletes than school teachers. On campus, you've been steeped in the study of a political science that stresses ideas and issues; out here, you'll find our politics dominated by money, media and image-managers. In the academic world, you have been encouraged to speak out, experiment and innovate; in the business world, you may be required to shut up, follow established policy and avoid making waves.

You've learned, in the last four years, to budget your time and your money and live within your means; you now will become a taxpayer supporting a government that makes a mockery of such values. You have studied enough history to know that the tides of time reflect the ebb and flow of war and peace, conflict and co-operation among nations. But now we are on the uncharted seas of the nuclear age, where every conflict could drift toward the ultimate shipwreck for humanity.

This has placed an unprecedented premium on the need to seek understanding and accommodation among competing interests and cultures — qualities that I think you and your classmates possess — even as leaders of nations appear to be turning toward confrontation. You would spend our national treasure on the tools for a better life; we are pouring it into more instruments for total death.

All of this, written down so coldly, can be depressing. But don't let the folly of your elders smother the spirit of youth. The world may be a wreck, it's true, but perhaps not yet an unredeemable wreck.

More than ever, the world needs what you have to offer — enthusiasm, idealism, hope and compassion. These are values that old cynics secretly envy, but will seek to snuff out lest their cynicism be seen for what it is rather than for the worldly wisdom they pretend it to be. Don't buy into the warped values of a weary world. Bring us your brightness, your vision and your concern for others, and force us to remember that we, too, shared your outlook once, and help us see that it is not too late to learn from the young.

Lovingly, Your father

The family gathers at Coe College, Cedar Rapids, Iowa, for the graduation of daughter Gini, center. Dad was commencement speaker. From left: Son-in-law Tom Shoop, Julie, Chris, dad, Marcy, Gini, Joan, Beth, Michael.

27

A LETTER TO A DAUGHTER
ON HER WEDDING DAY

The Des Moines Sunday Register, June 22, 1986

Dear Julie:

I am writing this shortly before having to walk you down the aisle at your wedding, and by the time you and everyone else reads this, it will be too late to change your mind. If you have any second thoughts now, please don't tell me about them.

It's been a long time since I've been in a wedding — 25 years, to be exact — so I have had a lot of time to think about marriage and its consequences. You are one of the six marvelous living consequences of the marriage that your mother and I are still working on. As the first of our children to marry, you are making a statement that what you have seen of the institution is not terribly frightening, and for that vote of confidence we thank you.

You might think that after a quarter-century of experience I would be filled with sage matrimonial advice and deep insight into this most mysterious of human relationships. You might think that, but you'd be disappointed. I'm not sure I can offer any wisdom, but I would like to offer hope.

Our society doesn't offer the newly married enough hope. Instead, it offers them plenty of reasons for doubt about marriage: financial pressures, the tensions of two-career couples, the difficulty of raising kids in the drug-sex-MTV age, the idea that changing mates is no more significant than changing

> **In every stone, there is a masterpiece waiting to be set free by loving, determined hands.**

jobs. Bombarded by such ideas, it's a wonder that anybody gets married today. Yet they do, but I wonder if many know what they're getting into. Remember, a few weeks ago, I told a graduating class that "Life Isn't High School"? Well, today's message is: Marriage Isn't Trivial Pursuit.

I've been trying to think of some metaphor that works. This one isn't perfect, but it makes a point: Getting married is like being given a huge, rectangular block of stone, a hammer and a chisel. There's a beautiful monument to love in there somewhere, if only you and your partner can work together to get it out.

This takes time and patience. You chip away at the formless stone for a while and when you tire, you hand the tools to your partner and he chips away. If you talk a lot while you work at it, you can develop a common vision of what it is you are going to shape. If you work separately and privately, you run the risk of shaping a two-headed monster, and soon you will hate what you're creating.

As you are working at it, you'll look around and see others couples sculpting. Some want everything at once. They hammer away in a frenzy for a while, but they have no staying power; they get frustrated and quit.

Others spy a fault-line in the stone — some flaw in their partner that they can't abide — and pick at it until it utterly shatters. Watch out for the fault lines. There are some in every marriage. You can work around them, maybe even incorporate the flaws into the design to add a touch of color or whimsy, but don't hammer at them.

There may be times, usually after same years of effort, when you will stand back and look at what you and your partner have shaped, and you will be dissatisfied. This is where many marriages end, and why our society's landscape is littered with the stone-cold ruins of divorce.

This is where you will need the long view of the artist who thinks not in terms of the moment but of a life's work. Here the essentials are vision and discipline. The vision must be of a masterpiece, worthy of a lifetime of effort. At any point in time it is unfinished, perhaps disappointing, but always potentially a masterpiece.

The discipline comes in setting your hearts and minds to achieving the masterpiece, knowing the reward in the end is worth the pain along the way.

After 25 years, your mother and I think we're about halfway finished. Our hands now grip the chisel and the hammer with familiar ease. The stone is yielding a pleasing form. With perhaps another quarter-century of shaping and polishing, God willing, we may finish our monument.

I can assure you it's worth the effort. In every stone, there is a masterpiece waiting to be set free by loving, determined hands. It is a lifetime's commitment, but I know that you and Tom are ready for it.

With pride and joy, Dad

At Graduation, a Father and Son Face the Future

The Des Moines Sunday Register, May 13, 1986

He is 22 years old, a fraternity man ready to leave the campus and take on the world. His degree in computer engineering from Iowa State University is a ticket to the fast track that runs from Silicon Valley in California to Route 128 in Boston. He waits impatiently at the starting line of adult life.

The past few weeks have been a whirlwind for my son Michael. He sent a resume and a carefully crafted letter to nearly 100 prospective employers, and the phone rarely stopped ringing after that. He had the kind of education that is the Information Society's better mousetrap, and the world beat a path to his door.

The companies flew him around the country to places where the computer generation works: San Diego, Sacramento, Denver, Dallas, Minneapolis, Boston. They pretended that they were interviewing him; in reality, he was interviewing them. Several offers came, and he agonized over the decision. He finally picked a Boston company that pretty much let him decide what kind of work he'd do.

He will graduate next Saturday in Ames, Iowa, and his dad and mom and brother and sisters will be there. He will be one of 2,850 graduates, virtually anonymous in the huge coliseum crowd, but his family will see him as if he were standing on a stage alone, the only

> His father, who nearly flunked freshman algebra at age 14 and swore off mathematics after that, does not understand where the young man got his talent.

31

person ever to conquer the mysteries of computer engineering.

His father, who nearly flunked freshman algebra at age 14 and swore off mathematics after that, does not understand where the young man got his talent. The kid always had a mastery of numbers, and after he bought his first computer as a high-school sophomore, the future career path became clear. The old man lived in a world of words, steeped in history, politics and today's news; the young man was up to his peripherals in digits, megabytes and programs.

It's all a mystery to the old man, but he's sure that the son is in the right place at the right time. He remembers that scene from "The Graduate," where the guy corners Dustin Hoffman at the graduation party and whispers one word — "plastics" — into college graduate's ear. The old man is tempted to walk around whispering "computer engineering" in the ears of all young people he meets, but they probably would give him that weird Dustin Hoffman look, so he just smiles quietly, knowing that one smart young man figured it all out himself, without being whispered to.

It's amazing, when you think about it, how these young people figure out what they're going to do, and then they find ways to do it. They seem to know a lot better than their parents or their peers what they are supposed to do, and advice is largely irrelevant. The old man, a dusty romantic suspicious of anything invented after World War II, probably would have steered the son into some dinosaur industry of galloping obsolescence. But the young man did not need advice — he had seen the future, and knew it was going to work for him.

Michael and his mom.

The father takes quiet satisfaction in the clear vision of the son, and the young man's persistence in pursuing it. He thinks now of his own decision 30 years ago, to break away and chart his own course as a journalist, and how he worried at the time whether his dad, a grain merchant, really approved. He loved words, just as his son loves numbers, and he knew he wanted to witness and write of the important events of his time, just as the son now wants to invent the future.

He came to understand, in time, that his own father

took great pride and satisfaction in his accomplishments as a journalist, and he knows that, in time, his son the computer engineer will know of his father's immense pride in him.

It's too bad the old grain merchant isn't around to see the journalist's son emerge as the computer engineer. He would think of the generational line they stood in — stretching from the Irish immigrant pioneer to the prairie farmer to the grain merchant, the journalist and now the computer whiz — and he would have seen it as the story of our century and our country.

And though the father tends to think of it as unique, it is a story being played out in millions of families this spring, as the rites of graduation send out another new generation of Americans to forge their futures. It is a time to celebrate their promise, and to remember how sweet it was to be 22, and at the threshold of a new world.

THE COST OF SAVING MY KIDS ILLUSTRATES THE HEALTH-CARE CRISIS

The Detroit News, March 22, 1992

Despite all I had read and heard about the health-care cost crisis, I didn't really understand until two of my children needed life-saving care after an automobile accident. The head-on crash last January 2 on a rural Virginia highway severely injured my 20-year-old son Chris, who was driving, and my 15-year-old daughter, Marcy. Both were in "code blue" condition, with survival uncertain, so the rescue squads called a helicopter to rush them 60 miles to a hospital in Fairfax, Virginia, near our home.

About an hour after the collision, Chris and Marcy were heading for surgery. My son's operation lasted 10 hours. My daughter's was spread over two days because their arrival with such serious injuries overtaxed Fairfax Hospital's emergency room facilities.

Heroic effort, the best technology and superbly talented doctors and nurses saved their lives. I have nothing but admiration and gratitude for the people who went all-out for my kids. Whatever it cost, it was worth that and much, much more. To watch my children recover is to be reminded that they are priceless.

> **My kids' hospital bill shouldn't be padded by 30 percent to cover the system's failures.**

I can still feel that way, however, and be amazed at what their care cost — and baffled by how our health-care system will survive its financial crisis.

Health-care costs are numbing when expressed in the billions of dollars involved but become dramatic when translated into figures the average person understands. I don't grasp billions, but I get the picture when a hospital bill shows a 30-minute helicopter ride cost $2,329 for each of my children. That $4,658 total is approximately the value of Chris' wrecked car.

Chris was treated for multiple fractures of both legs, a broken collarbone, and various cuts and bruises. Here's a sample of his hospital charges:

- Intensive care, two days — $2,016
- Semiprivate room, 13 days — $3,367.
- Medical-surgical supplies — $9,230.
- Operating room services — $7,074
- Anesthesia supplies — $2,559.
- Pharmacy — $3,461.
- Physical therapy: — $ 1,484.

The list goes on and on, and the bottom line came to $43,892. And that's just for the hospital. The orthopedic surgeon's bill for $18,500 arrived the other day. Marcy's hospital bill was $26,325 for eight days' care.

The bills, still coming in, exceed $90,000 so far — more than it would cost to send Marcy to Harvard for four years and buy Chris a new car. Luckily, our health insurance will cover nearly everything. But about 35 million Americans lack medical coverage — and their kids get sick or hurt, too. What happens when they face such huge bills? The answer is that insured patients cover their bills, or our employers get stuck with them in the premiums they pay.

Fairfax Hospital wouldn't have turned away my kids if they'd been uninsured. They would have passed on the costs to paying customers. That's what hospitals do. It's called "cost shifting," and it works like a hidden tax on those who pay their own bills or have insurance. Chris and Marcy's hospital bills were padded by about 30 percent to cover the facility's costs from uninsured patients or Medicare and Medicaid beneficiaries, who don't pay full costs.

"If everyone paid, and paid the same, we could take about 30 percent off our charges," said Richard Magenheimer, a vice-president at Fairfax Hospital. Michael Bromberg, executive director of the Federation of American Health Systems, a trade association, explained: "There's a hidden tax on you that is used by the hospital to care for the next person who doesn't have health insurance. The middle-class subsidizes the poor, and it's reached the point where it's almost abusive."

This is a system careening toward collapse. It is unjust, unfair and out of control. Every American should have basic health insurance. My kids' hospital bill shouldn't be padded by 30 percent to cover the system's failures. We're avoiding taxes for universal health coverage by paying the hidden tax of cost-shifting. This is the price we pay for supporting politicians who coin phrases like "no new taxes."

Our children taught us courage amid pain and crisis

The Detroit News, January 3, 1993

Let us now hail the coming of 1993, for surely it comforts us to bid good-bye and good riddance to 1992. Like a bad wine, 1992 had the taste of a vintage best forgotten. Admittedly, this is a highly personal view born of intensely personal experience. For many others, 1992 may be a year to be savored. For our family, it was the dregs.

The year was just one day old when I knew it would be memorably miserable. On January 2 a year ago, I watched from the side of a highway while rescue workers extracted my son and daughter from the wreckage of a head-on collision. All I could think of was the nightmarish prospect of planning a funeral for one — or two — of my children.

That picture is the one my memory will call up when the year 1992 comes to mind. But that freeze-frame captures only the most stunning moment, not the year's true meaning. As it evolved, 1992 was like a slow-motion morality play that began with a crisis and resolved itself, step by painful step, into a story of courage and survival.

Our children supplied the courage. Twenty-year-old Christopher and 15-year-old Marcy used their broken bones and their pain as teaching tools, giving the rest of the family a deeply moving lesson in the graceful acceptance of adversity. Without complaining, without questioning why God distributes misfortune so haphazardly, they poured their energies into healing. In so doing, they healed us all.

The crutches and the casts, the surgeries and the therapy, are all behind them now — like homely pieces of a jigsaw puzzle that somehow come together to form a picture of startling loveliness.

It is too much for parents to expect stoic courage and selfless maturity from young people whom they still may regard — perhaps unfairly — as "me-generation" teen-agers. When these qualities emerge under the severe test of pain and disrupted lives, we realize that our "kids" have a strength and depth of character that we had never suspected.

But the kids learned, too, how valuable parents can be. We were no longer just the old grumps imposing rules and discouraging fun. We were there to empty the bedpans and change the bandages, serve the meals, drive to the doctor, rent the video movies, run their errands and just sit and sympathize when there was nothing more useful to do.

When you have listened at hospital bedside to the concussion-induced babbling of a teen-age daughter who thinks she is 4 years old, how wonderful it is when her mind clears and she becomes a teen-ager again. It gives a parent a new appreciation for a phase of life that previously seemed only a phase to endure.

When you have felt the strong arm of your tall son over your shoulder, leaning on you as he struggles to learn to walk again, you have experienced the satisfaction of being really needed as a father. This is something you will remember — and more important, that he will remember — one day when you need someone to lean on.

On Christmas Eve, when the family gathered around the holiday punch bowl, it was Christopher who wanted to propose the toast. He had us raise our glasses in praise of what we'd all been through, noting with feeling that the year had shown us how precious is the gift of a loving family. No one could have said it better.

When I think of 1992, I will think of Charles Dickens' famous line: "It was the best of times. It was the worst of times." So let it be — both a year to forget and a year to remember.

To Fathers, The Heroes We May Have Missed

The Detroit News, June 18, 1989

Somewhere among the faded photographs that lie aging in an antique steamer trunk at home, there is a picture of a young man in a baseball uniform. He is tall, lanky and agile, a natural first baseman. He wears a uniform cut and styled with the look of the World War I era, bearing the name of the "East Side Athletics." The man has coal-black hair, slicked back straight, with the sheen of Vaseline. He is young and strong and handsome.

The image of the photo leaped to mind the other night when I went to see the movie Field of Dreams. I went expecting a diverting fantasy about baseball. I didn't realize it would bring back my father so vividly.

The film concerns an Iowa farmer named Ray Kinsella who converts a cornfield to a lighted baseball diamond after hearing a voice say: "If you build it, he will come." The farmer believes that somehow, his magic baseball field will lure back to life the legendary Shoeless Joe Jackson, a tragic figure in the 1919 Black Sox scandal, who had been a hero to his dead father.

> **One of life's sad facts is that most of us know our fathers only as older men.**

Shoeless Joe was banned from professional baseball for life, along with several Chicago White Sox teammates, as punishment for conspiring to lose the 1919 World Series. Forever after, they were the Black Sox — baseball's damned.

My father was 30 years old in 1919, an avid baseball fan, and I recall him talking of Shoeless Joe and the Black Sox. He also spoke of other major league greats of the period — Ty Cobb, Walter Johnson, Tris Speaker, and, the great double-play men, Tinkers-to-Evers-to-Chance. To me, they were just names of long-dead players who wore funny-looking caps and baggy pants. To him, they were heroes of his youth, contemporaries that he long outlived but remembered vividly.

The film's Iowa farmer and I have a lot in common. Our fathers played baseball in that era of daytime games on real grass, and we heard their endless, repetitive tales of Shoeless Joe's hitting, Cobb's spikes-up base stealing and Johnson's curve ball. But at the time, they were just stories told by gray-haired men with long memories and foolish dreams.

It isn't until late in the movie that it becomes clear that the story isn't about baseball or Shoeless Joe or the ball diamond in the cornfield. It is, instead, about the regret of sons who never knew their fathers as the young men they once were.

One of life's sad facts is that most of us know our fathers only as older men. We never knew them in the full promise of their youth, in their days of slicked-back black hair, with the glint of unlimited possibilities in bright, eager eyes. We came to know them after life had dealt out enough of its hardness to diminish their dreams and reduce their hopes to some lower common denominator of reality.

That was especially true in my case, as my dad was just one month shy of 50 years old when I was born. He was born a century ago, in 1889 — just two years after Shoeless Joe, though he outlived him by nearly a quarter-century. Lucky for me that he did, or I might have few memories of him at all. I knew him as a vigorous but aging man with white hair, a business executive in a gray suit and white shirt, not a lanky first-baseman in a baseball uniform.

When I discovered that old East Side Athletics picture years ago, it was a shock to see him in the black-haired vigor of his playing days, a young man who looked like he could beat out a bunt for a single or stretch a two-bagger into a triple. He looked as athletic as Shoeless Joe, a graceful left fielder whose glove was called "the place where triples go to die."

At the climax of Field of Dreams, Ray Kinsella's father appears on the magic ball field as the strong, young catcher with big league dreams. "Is it him?" Ray's wife asks. "I'm not sure," Kinsella replies, "I never knew him when he was a young man."

So it is with most of us. This summer, my father would have turned 100. On Father's Day, I'll think about his tales of Shoeless Joe, told by a man who saw himself as a black-haired first baseman — a man, to my eternal regret, that I never really knew.

2

DOWN ON THE FARM

"With all its history and memories, the farm is mine now. You could say I own it, and the legal document says I do, but the funny thing about the land is that you don't really own it. We're all tenants on the land, and transients in time, leaving our names on yellowing pieces of paper that do nothing to alter the land and its timeless promise."

Of Ghosts, broken dreams, and the promise of the land

The Des Moines Sunday Register, April 27, 1980

Some 40 miles south of Des Moines, in the northeast corner of Clarke County, there is a 160-acre farm in a sad state of neglect. The house, roughly a half-century old, is forlornly vacant and vandalized. The windows have been shot out, the porch is sagging, the doors have been broken in.

The barn, a pale gray shadow of the strong red structure it once was, groans and creaks in the wind, its doors either missing or hanging limply on rusted, tired hinges. There are two or three other sad outbuildings and a farmyard collection of cast-off washing machines, bed springs, stove pipes, broken-handled shovels and other mute reminders of people who have come and gone from these acres. It's a small slice of Appalachia, incongruously plunked down in these rolling pastures and fields of south-central Iowa. And it's mine.

> Don't ask what a city-slicker transplanted to Iowa from the East is doing with a farm that looks like it's on welfare.

Don't ask what a city-slicker transplanted to Iowa from the East is doing with a farm that looks like it's on welfare. The answer is so complicated that I haven't really sorted it out yet, except that I know it has as much to do with mysticism and romance as with economics and realism. I can't tell a pesticide from a herbicide, and I can't operate any machine more complicated than a typewriter, but the land has a lure that is magic and magnetic, a promise of permanence and roots and hope that I do not find in anything else.

Farmer Jim and his Iowa corn.

I spent a warm, sunny afternoon on the land last week and decided that, despite its first-glance look of Appalachian poverty, the place has a barely concealed richness and beauty that are ready to be groomed and revealed.

There's a little orchard of fruit trees, choked in brambles and the dry stalks of last year's weeds, that's on the verge of exploding into blossoms of apple and pear. There's a still, hidden pond, where the frogs are practicing their spring-song, and a woodpecker is hammering out machine-gun messages on a hollow, dead tree. There's a hilltop ready for corn and a broad, flat bottomland ready for soybeans, and a creek that snakes through a woods on the back forty. There's a silence in the afternoon that lets you hear the wind coming from afar, a wind you can hear coming before you feel it blow across the dusty road and into the barn, where it sets the boards to complaining.

And all about the place, there is a feeling of the past, an echo of men working the fields and wives hanging the wash and children playing in the dust of the driveway. I got to wondering about that past, and about the ghosts and broken dreams that I may have inherited with this place, so I dug out a rolled-up legal document called an abstract of title, which came to me when I bought the farm. It tells a story that only reinforces the feeling that the land itself seems to exhale.

The old papers, yellowed and dry, say that the United States of America granted this land to a Joseph Duvall in October of 1860. Lincoln was about to be elected president, the Civil War was brewing, and Joseph Duvall was hacking a homestead out of what must have been a remote wooded corner of a new state. The abstract records a bewildering trail of transactions down through the years — the land was bought and sold, divided, added to, passed on to heirs of various families, sold for delinquent taxes and squabbled over among various claimants. The land stayed, but the people came and went, just so many transients passing through time.

Like a tiny mirror of history, the abstract reflects time and trouble, poignantly capturing the tragedy of the Great Depression. In its stilted legal jargon, it records the harsh demands of one A.F. Wade, holder of an $8,500 mortgage on the farm, who in February 1931 asked the county court to declare the owner, a widow named Nan Johnson, in default for failing to make the mortgage payments. This Mr. Wade demanded that the land be sold to satisfy the debt, and further asked that 330 bushels of corn and 100 bushels of oats, raised on the land in 1931, be declared his, along with any crops raised in 1932.

A judge named H.H. Carter found the widow in default and ordered the place sold. The document tells that the sheriff, Tom Stancell, went out to the farm on December 30, 1931, and informed the widow's tenants, Andrew and Pansy Goodrich, that the place was about to be sold and that they should get out. Happy New Year, Andrew and Pansy.

And so on January 23, 1933, in that darkest hour of the Depression, after the American people had repudiated Herbert Hoover but had not yet witnessed the inauguration of hope with Franklin Roosevelt, the farm was put on the auction block. It went up for sale at 10 o'clock in the morning at the east door of the county courthouse in Osceola, and Sheriff Stancell first offered it for sale in parcels, but there were no bidders. Finally, he offered the whole place as a unit, and there was one bidder ~ A.F. Wade, the man with the mortgage, got the place for $4,000.

After World War II, the land passed to other hands, to a family named Parker, which held it for 30 years. And the last person to live here, a bachelor named Ned Parker, lived alone, until one day he killed himself.

With all its history and memories, the farm is mine now. You could say I own it, and the legal document says I do, but the funny thing about the land is that you don't really own it. We're all tenants on the land, and transients in time, leaving our names on yellowing pieces of paper that do nothing to alter the land and its timeless promise.

And so I will work on the place, seeking to erase its Appalachian look and hoping to learn something in the process. Don't ask me why. It just seems the right thing to do.

THE AWESOME POWER OF AN IOWA HAILSTORM

Des Moines Sunday Register, June 22, 1980

From a half-mile away, we could tell that something was wrong — very seriously wrong — at the farm. It seemed that we sensed it before we really saw it. I knew when we reached the farm we would be confronted by something we didn't want to see, but from a half-mile away, it was only a shapeless fear and a subliminal perception.

> **It is the sort of whipping that the gods of the angry skies have been administering with frightening regularity this spring, all across Iowa.**

You could see from that distance that the old barn was standing, which in a way was reassuring, but still the landscape and horizon looked all wrong. Then, as we turned into the farm, the realization hit like news of sudden death. It. was the trees. The trees were bare. It is the middle of June, the season of life, and all the leaves were gone from all the trees.

They stood there, unseasonably naked, reaching to the sky with wounded limbs. Some of the smaller branches were broken and dangling, and there were gouges in the bark where the light-colored flesh of the living wood showed through. One little tree on the edge of the driveway looked like it had been chained to a post and lashed with a whip.

This particular whipping occurred last weekend, as a fierce wind and hail storm swooped down on the northeast corner of Clarke County, where a naive newspaperman not long ago purchased a rundown old farm. It is the sort of whipping that the gods of the angry skies have been administering with frightening regularity this spring, all across Iowa. Hailstorms have become part of the Iowa routine in recent weeks, and the Iowa farmer is reaching into his reserve of stoic strength to deal with the loss, and the naive newspaperman is learning the need for stoic strength.

As my wife Joan and I surveyed the damage, the intensity of the storm became clear. The old house, which is vacant, told part of the story. All the windows on the north and west were broken — even the big, double-paned picture window under the overhang of the front porch. The hail had to be flying almost horizontally to hit it. The roof looked as if it had been machine-gunned. The new yellow paint on the old wood siding was pock-marked, and a gallon paint can on the porch was dented deeply.

The barn siding was pitted, as if someone had stood back in the barnyard and blasted it with a giant shotgun. The windows were gone — glass, frames and all — and from inside you could look up and see a checkerboard sky peeking through the places where the shingles blew away.

We walked silently. In one place, the top edges of a board fence were chewed away, as if some tall, hungry rodent had been at work. In another

Hail broke windows and shredded shingles on the old farmhouse.

place, whole boards had been ripped off the posts.

There was nothing in the fields, of course. Where the foot-tall corn had been a week earlier, there was bare ground. What seemed most incredible, though, was that you couldn't see a trace of the corn plants. There weren't any of those battered stalks you see in the newspaper pictures of hail damage. There was nothing, except some residue from last year's crop — chunks of stalks and corncobs.

Over in the old orchard, the young apples were pounded into the ground, and for the first time, you could see through the orchard clear out to the road because there wasn't a leaf to obscure the vision.

Gradually, a rather eerie feeling developed. "This is spooky," Joan said, and I agreed. Looking down by the pond, where some big oaks stood with that stark mid-winter look on a warm June evening, we both agreed we'd never seen anything like it. The farm now was out of sync with the season — the brown, bare fields and naked trees said it was December, but the calendar said it was June.

The farm had an altogether different look than at any time in the past. It was picked clean. Along the fence-rows, where weeds and vines had clung to the wire, even in winter, there was nothing. You could look down the fence lines and see clearly each strand of wire. Objects never before seen emerged from the fields — an old car battery, a rusted hay rake, a roll of wire fencing, a junk stove. They had always before been obscured by growth. Even the giant musk thistles, which have stalks an inch thick, were gone — chopped off a few inches from the ground. The pastures looked as if a horde of locusts had swept through, eating them clean, except that the stubble remaining all leaned in one direction — southeast, flattened by the wind.

The enormity of the storm was written in one final symbol: the dead rabbits. We found one huddled near the old hay rake, as if it had been seeking cover, and another stretched out in open pasture. These were not frail little baby bunnies; they were big, healthy-looking adults. They had been pummeled to death by flying ice.

That was enough. We didn't want to see any more. We knew the soybean fields at the back of the farm would be bare, so we didn't bother to go look. We got back in the car and left. Later, I talked by telephone to the farmer next door, Howard Miller. He said he's been farming there for 40 years and had never been hit by hail before.

"It just stripped everything — there isn't a plant alive here," he said. "Everything is completely wiped out." The storm hit on Saturday evening, June 14, and it lasted about 45 minutes, Miller said. The wind was clocked at 75 miles per hour. "We had a terrible flood afterward," he said. "Our rain gauges were blown away, but I heard we had about five-and-a-half inches," which sent the creek over its banks and took down fences. Miller and his family retreated to the basement when the storm struck, and emerged later to find the kitchen piled high with some very odd hail. "Some of it was as big as your fist," he said. "But it didn't really look like hail to me — it was jagged, and some pieces were six to eight inches long. It was more like an ice storm."

"A lot of birds and rabbits are dead, and a lot of pheasants. I was afraid it might have killed some of my cattle, but I went out after the storm to check them and they just acted like they were wore out — just tired," he said. "I thought it was going to blow the house away, " he added. 'Every roof on the place has to be replaced'—house, barn, sheds and all.

How was he taking it? "There isn't a whole lot of good humor down here right now," he remarked. But he is already re-roofing and replanting. "It's just one of those things — no way to stop it," he said, in a classic example of Iowa stoicism.

One more call filled out the picture. It was from Don Russell, a professional farm manager who oversees the naive newspaperman's farm. Russell is a veteran in the business, an expert who has seen hail damage all over Iowa for many years. "Your farm is he worst hail damage I have ever seen — ever," Russell said. It's no financial tragedy for me; farming isn't my livelihood. But it makes you marvel, and admire the Iowans who pour all of the labor, resources and hope into the soil, and manage to bounce back, again and again, when misfortune knocks them down.

THE COLLAPSE OF THE FARM ECONOMY: IF IT WERE A CITY PROBLEM, THERE WOULD BE RIOTS

The Des Moines Sunday Register September 25, 1985

Only a few old-timers remember "the Roaring Twenties." The 1920s saw a boom of speculation and wealth-building. It was a decade of prosperity for many Americans — but not for farmers. Agriculture was left out of the Roaring Twenties, just as it seems left out of the prosperity enjoyed by many in the Easy Eighties.

While America went on a binge of speculation in stocks during the 1920s, creating the myth of instant riches, something drastically different was happening down on the farm. In rural America, wealth created in the World War I boom was disappearing, just as now, after the Speculative Seventies.

> **Nobody wants to see that happen, but if it did, some old-timers would say, "I told you so."**

The price of Iowa farmland peaked in 1921 at $235 an acre. Then it began falling — and kept falling, and kept falling — not for three or five or even 10 years, but for 12 straight years. It went down as if there were no bottom: to $155 in 1926, to $117 in 1931, to $69 in 1933. After having fallen to less than one-third of its 1921 value, Iowa farmland didn't return to that level until 1958.

Iowans who thought they were rich as the '20s began were desperately poor as the decade ended And another generation of farmers that thought itself wealthy at the end of the '70s is sliding toward poverty now.

The price of Iowa land has fallen 49 percent, on average, since 1981. There is no bottom in sight. We don't know whether the decline is nearly over, or gaining momentum. What if it goes on for another five or seven years?

As the slide continues, it sucks more and more farm families into the whirlpool. It pulled in the bad farmers first — the reckless debtors and bad managers who some say deserve their fate— but they are long gone. Now it's pulling down Iowa's best people, the solid citizens of the countryside, who don't deserve to lose their land, their heritage and their hope just because their leaders are too dumb or too insensitive to understand, care and act.

If you are a city person and you can't quite relate to this, think of it this way: Suppose that $80,000 home you bought five years ago was worth less than $41,000 today (that's a 49-per-cent decline). Suppose further that you have a $68,000 mortgage on it, your payments are $900 a month and your income in the last three years has declined by about half.

Do you think you'd feel desperate? Do you think you'd be screaming bloody murder at the government to do something to prevent you and all your neighbors from losing your homes? You bet you would.

Iowans are taking this disaster with a kind of stoic fatalism one might expect of the meek who had inherited the Earth. If it were a city problem, there would be riots. But don't be too complacent, city people — this bell yet may toll for thee.

Urban people who watched last Sunday's Farm Aid concert, amused at its quaint appeals for charity for farmers, may not understand that the widening depression in agriculture could threaten them, too. "You can't put a wall around it," commented Michael Boehlje, assistant dean of Iowa State University's College of Agriculture, at last week's Iowa bankers convention.

The Iowa State economist likened the farm crisis to a series of waves. The first wave washed out the debt-ridden farmers. A second wave is undermining financially strong farmers by eroding the value of their land and machinery. A third wave has hit rural communities, where retail sales are down and bills are going unpaid and loans are going delinquent at stores and banks.

A fourth wave will hit the entire nation, Boehlje predicts, "when financial institutions — banks, insurance companies and the Farm Credit system — start encountering problems." That wave now looms on the horizon, threatening job losses, financial stresses and debt problems all across the American economy.

President Ronald Reagan may not understand the crisis in agriculture, but he probably would get the message if the Bank of America becomes threatened with failure. It may take the threat of a general financial crisis to drive the message home in Washington. Nobody wants to see that happen, but if it did, some old-timers would say, "I told you so." For they remember the Roaring Twenties. And we all know what followed.

Farm wives reveal the grief behind the mask of tranquility

The Des Moines Sunday Register, October 20, 1985

Something sad and strange and scary seems to be happening in the weeks following the Farm Aid concert, which focused national attention on the plight of America's farm families. I've noticed it in the increasing amount of mail received from depressed and fearful farm women, who are watching the men in their lives crumble under the pressure of the farm crisis.

I don't know if that heavily covered media event had anything to do with it, but something has triggered an outpouring of grief and worry by the wives of Iowa farmers who are at the edge of a financial and personal crisis. The letters I'm receiving from these Iowa farm homes — nearly always written by the women, not the men — have a tone of desperation.

> **"Some nights my 67-year-old husband and I just lie in bed and weep until we howl."**

The men are supposed to be strong and stoic and silent. They do not spill out the hidden fear and shame to anyone but the women in their lives. That leaves the woman carrying the burden for them both, and some need to share it with any sympathetic listener they can find. For some, it is too bitter a story to share with friends and relatives, so they share it with a stranger.

"Some nights my 67-year-old husband and I just lie in bed and weep until we howl," wrote an Eastern Iowa farm wife. "Everything my husband | worked so hard for all these years is down the drain. Our beautiful house, which we planned on retiring in, is now for sale for $40,000 less than it is worth, and I

55

scramble to find housing for us in our old age. All of our farms are for sale, and we're accepting less than what we paid for them. By selling everything, my husband's son hopes to be able to still farm by renting land."

The letter, neatly typed on pink paper, continues: "My husband, once a proud man, is reduced to humbling himself at our (four generation) bank, and begs for money. Where we were once invited to parties given by the bank for their larger depositors, and given free football tickets, we now find when we ask for help for finding a home, to go 'find an apartment to rent!' The friendly banker has deserted us.

"Sept. 28th we saw two lawyers skilled in insolvency. They give us advice as to our procedure, and we sleep for the first time in weeks. For a farmer of our size they ask $16,000 to $20,000 for our case. We ask, 'Would you take some lots?'

"Farmers are a proud bunch, and few know how badly we are hurting financially, for the farm crisis is talked about only in general terms. I tell my husband that I will look funny in bankruptcy court in my mink jacket — a purchase [that] now haunts me, for when can I wear it with all of our farmer friends hurting financially. . . Thanks for listening. Pray for us. It indeed all looks so hopeless!"

The farm crisis has received massive media coverage, yet I doubt most Americans or even most Iowans comprehend the sense of desperation that now grips many farm families. It hit me in talking with farm people who rode our Farm Aid Express train. Some grasped at the train ride as a way to escape the grief and reach out to others who might understand and care.

"I've never ridden a train before," wrote one farm wife, "and I felt relaxed and comfortable, and for a few hours forgot about what would be at home when we returned. The same stress, the same debts, still due and waiting for us, and the same fear in our neighbors' eyes, wondering who would be going under next.

"I did a lot of thinking on that train, as I watched people and looked out the windows. . . I noticed many farm houses, and I wondered which were in trouble, and which, if any, weren't. I wondered about the farm women and the children and how other people were dealing with the problems that my family is so familiar with. . . I hope they keep their families together and hold on to their pride and self-esteem. . .

"I carried an American Agriculture hat with me to give to Willie Nelson, but I couldn't even get close to him. I wanted so badly to shake his hand and just say thanks for a great concert and for caring about people like me."

Last week, as I drove across Iowa on a brilliant autumn day, I wondered which of the farmhouses sheltered such grieving women, and which of the combines in the fields were driven by desperate men. It all looked so prosperous and peaceful as the huge harvest was being gathered. But behind its tranquil mask, the face of rural Iowa is streaked with tears.

A Santa Claus for Iowa

The Des Moines Sunday Register, December 22, 1985

Yes, Iowa, there is a Santa Claus. His name is Herman, and he lives in Cincinnati.

His first letter to me arrived early in December. He wrote that he wanted to help a needy Iowa farm family with a gift of $1,000. "While I realize that the amount offered is but a drop in the bucket, it is hoped that it might replace despair and discouragement with hope and faith for one farm family," the letter said. "I am a retired federal employee whose monthly annuity is $832, so you can see that I am not living 'high off the hog.'... But I have only one mouth to feed and, thank God, have reasonably good health," he wrote. "All things considered, Jesus Christ has blessed me real good."

> Yes, Iowa, there is a Santa Claus. His name is Herman, and he lives in Cincinnati.

The letter made two requests: that I find a farm family needing help, and that I not reveal the donor's name. It sounded nice, but was it for real? Not many people write editors asking for help in giving their money away. Skeptical, I called a Cincinnati number listed in Herman's name.

Why are you doing this, Herman?

It was the faces of the Iowa farm children he saw on television news that moved him, he said. The news account reported the dreadful toll of the farm financial crisis in Iowa — suicides, family breakups, stress. "I saw kids working with a therapist, and that really got to me," he said.

OK, Herman, but why did you write to me?

After seeing the TV program, he went to the library to read more about the farm problem. He ran across my name in an article about The Register's Farm Aid Express, that trainload of Iowa farm people that we hauled to Willie Nelson's big Farm Aid concert last fall. I was quoted as saying there's a feeling in Iowa that the rest of the country doesn't really give a damn about farmers' problems. But Herman does, and he wanted to prove it.

"I just feel I should help," he said. "I'm 66, and I better do something worthwhile before I leave this Earth. The Lord laid it on my heart to help someone. I know $1,000 isn't going to cure anything, but it could give them hope. It might renew their hope and keep them going. Whoever receives the money, they will know that someone does care."

Herman is a former tax collector — a retired IRS agent. He's also an Army veteran of combat in North Africa, Italy and Sicily. "I should have been killed on the Anzio beach in World War II, but Christ saved my life." Herman was for real.

Calls to organizations working with distressed farm families quickly produced an abundance of candidates for Herman's gift. We need 10,000 secret Santas like him, I thought. Why is there only one?

I didn't like the job of picking one family — too much like playing God, But Herman needed a name; he wanted his help to be person-to-person, or, as he put it, "stranger-to-stranger." So I called him back and told him about the Roger Taylor family of Dickens. Roger, 39, is a severe diabetic, with no money for insulin. His wife, Kathy, 37, has a kidney disease. Their son Jarrod, 11, cashed in his savings bonds to help pay the family's utility bills. The Taylors have already lost most of their 400 acres of land in northwest Iowa.

Herman said he was on the way to his bank. Two days later, an express package arrived at my desk, containing a $1,000 bank-cashier's check made out to young Jarrod Taylor, and a letter to the sixth-grader who had sacrificed for his family.

"Use the money for whatever purpose you wish," Herman wrote to Jarrod. "You and your family must never, never, never give in to despair, discouragement and frustration, no matter how bad things look...."May God bless your family this Christmas with the hope of better things for the new year. Jarrod, one | day you will look back on these dark days and say to your children, 'We never gave up — for we always knew we'd make it."

In a second letter to me, Herman wrote that he hoped his act might inspire others. "Perhaps, by some miracle, our efforts might become contagious and produce a snowballing effect." But he again insisted on anonymity, quoting Matthew: "... when you do a charitable deed, do not sound a trumpet...."

Yes, Iowa, there is a Santa Claus. Thank you, Herman, for your gift — not the $1,000, but the hope, faith, and caring that all of us can share — and imitate.

THE CLOSING CHAPTER ON SHAMROCK FARM

The Des Moines Sunday Register, October 30, 1988

Every life is like a book. We write our own histories in our daily living, most of the time unconscious that each day is a thread in the story of our lives. Every so often, however, there are moments when we become aware that we are completing a chapter, turning a page. The chapter that I finished last week is titled Shamrock Farm. It began in 1980, shortly after I moved to Iowa, and it's subtitled, "The Education of a City Man."

I had never lived on a farm, nor known farm people well, having grown up in Minneapolis. I knew that nothing defined Iowa and its people more than the culture, economics and sociology of rural living. If I were to know and understand Iowa, I would need to know and understand agriculture and how it shaped its people.

And so I bought a farm. It would be a chance to live and learn something about what makes Iowa tick. There were other motives, of course. The land, especially in the rolling fields and patchy woods of southern Iowa, was beautiful, a peaceful and refreshing retreat from the stress of work. And then there was greed.

> **Farmers aren't paranoid; there really _are_ that many enemies.**

Iowa was in the midst of a land boom. Farmers, bankers and smart-money economists all were convinced that land prices could only go up — as they had since the early 1970s. One of Des Moines' best-known financial advisers urged me to invest in farmland. Borrow all the money you can, buy as much prime land as possible, and watch it double in five years, he advised. As an act of charity, he shall remain nameless.

Because of my low tolerance for debt and risk, I did not follow his advice fully. I bought poor land, cheap, with cash. The farm, in Clarke County, was 160 acres of neglect and hard luck. The buildings were falling down. The place was littered with rusting remains of every piece of machinery and metal scrap that ever crossed the front gate.

It was a farm that had driven more than one generation to bankruptcy, and one man to suicide. It was a place of ghosts and broken dreams. The barn creaked and groaned in the wind, whispering of past sorrows and failures. The empty house told tales of children, in broken toys, and of a farm wife, in the Mason jars still filled with preserved fruit that lay in the dust of a dark cellar. The once-fruitful orchard was now in the clutches of brambles and thistles.

Gradually, we restored the land's dignity. The machinery scrap was hauled away. Collapsing sheds were dismantled and burned. With sickle and sweat, fire and curses, we made war on the weeds and thorns, winning, in time, a scarred victory. We painted and re-roofed the barn. In a moment of spectacular folly, I torched the farm house. Lord, how it ended in a blaze of glory!

We fixed the fences, built a pond, bulldozed ditches to channel excess water, planted new grasses and alfalfa on the hill ground to conserve the soil. We share-cropped the land with hardworking tenants who raised corn, soybeans and hay. We suffered droughts and floods and one incredible hailstorm that gave the entire farm a half-inch crew cut while killing the rabbits and birds.

There were good years and bad years. We learned why farm people talk so much of the weather, the price of corn and the government farm program. We learned how fast your blood, sweat, toil and tears could go down the drain with a turn in the weather or a change in the rules or a slump in the export trade.

We learned how little control farmers have over their own fates. We began to understand their siege mentality — if it isn't the drought or the hail or the cornborer that's going to get you, it's the government or the Russians or the international bankers who manipulate the dollar. No, they aren't paranoid; there really are that many enemies.

After all the effort, all the improvement, and nine years of education, Shamrock Farm was worth slightly more than half what we paid for it. We sold the place a week ago, to good people who will care for it. As an investment, it was awful. As an education, it was like the Ivy League — the tuition was incredibly high, but the learning will last.

The chapter closes with this epilogue: Iowa, treasure your land, and cherish your farmers. They are your heart and soul.

3

ROOTS: MY IRISH THING

"And so I now live with an ethnic memory and a set of stories to live out. It is a memory of poverty and repression, a story of fierce determination to be independent and self-reliant. It is a memory of land lost and a story of new land reclaimed. It is a memory of people I never knew — peasants grubbing out potatoes on a half-acre of stony soil — who seem nearly as real as the people in my own story — kids with Irish freckles, some with red hair, who watch their father turn St. Patrick's Day into a celebration second only to Christmas."

In Search of My Irish Roots

The Wall Street Journal, September 21, 1977

The dark and brooding ruins of a Norman castle look down upon the village of Trim, in Ireland's County Meath. Crows circle its ancient tower, still standing tall after more than 750 years, as cows graze incongruously within the castle's walls. High in the rugged stone walls, two large windows peer open like eyes; they have seen my people, ages ago.

Thousands of miles away, in the valley of the Minnesota River, the rich black soil is carpeted by summer's green wealth of corn. The land rolls away from a big, white farmhouse in waves of green, cut into neat squares by gravel country roads. It is an inexhaustibly rich land. Inviting man's plow each spring and rewarding his labor each autumn with a recurring bounty that is more reliable and predictable than life itself.

The link between the two places is a man who came to know each as his home. The Norman castle was already 600 years old when Lawrence Gannon, my great-grandfather, was a boy in Trim. Perhaps he played within those walls, on that soil where I stood this summer, watching the crows circle overhead. The scene in 1827 may not have been much different from what it was in 1977; such ancient ruins mock our sense of time, and mark 150 years as we might mark 15.

The United States of America grants unto Lawrence Gannon a tract of 160 acres.

What drove the boy from Trim I do not know, nor what he left behind. The sketchy family records only show that he left Ireland around 1850, when the great out-migration caused by the potato famine was filling ships bound for America with thousands and thousands like him. Chances are he left little behind. In those overpopulated days of Ireland's direst poverty, the common folk scratched out a grim subsistence on tiny plots of land, more often rented than owned.

"Unless an Irish laborer could get hold of a patch of land and grow potatoes on which to feed himself and his children, the family starved," historian Cecil Woodham-Smith wrote in "The Great Hunger," her epic of the Irish Famine of 1845-49. "... As the population increased and the demand for a portion of ground grew more frantic, land became like gold in Ireland. ... The possession of a piece of land was literally the difference between life and death."

From this background of famine and land-hunger, Lawrence Gannon joined the stream of destitute Irish flowing to that vast promised land of America, with its endless horizons of frontier waiting to be populated. He landed in New York City, but the land-hunger stayed with him and drove him West.

Trim Castle

He had reached Ohio when he learned that land in Minnesota could be had from the federal government for free, merely by settling there and staking a claim. It was an Irishman's impossible dream: free land. The year was 1855, and Minnesota was still an Indian-troubled territory, but free land was enough to lure the Irish immigrant, his wife and four-year-old son to the north woods.

The Minnesota River was a main route west from St. Paul in those days, and it brought my ancestor to a village called Belle Plaine, founded by a French trader in 1852. He struck out into an area nearby known as "the big woods," and along with other Irish, German and Scandinavian immigrants, Lawrence Gannon turned the woods into open, fertile fields.

In the summer of 1976, I made my own journey down the Minnesota River — but on a four-lane highway that now runs parallel to it. With my 12-year-old son, Michael, sharing my roots-search, I stopped to dig into old land records in the county courthouse at Shakopee, Minnesota. There, in musty deed-books that date back to pioneer days, Lawrence Gannon's impossible dream is recorded in the elegant penmanship of that age.

The message fairly leapt out of the page at me: The United States of America grants unto Lawrence Gannon a tract of 160 acres. "In testimony whereof, I, Abraham Lincoln, President of the United States, have caused these letters to be made patent, and the seal of the General Land Office to be hereunto affixed." The paper is dated June 1, 1861.

The decree is so official, so final. "Now know ye, that there is therefore granted by the United States unto the said Lawrence Gannon and to his heirs, the tract of land above described: to have and to hold the said tract of land with the appurtenances thereof, unto the said Lawrence Gannon and to his heirs and assigns, forever."

"Forever."

It is a compelling word, one rarely used any more. In the mobile, transient, throw-away society which we live in, forever is a word that's becoming obsolete. No longer do marriages last forever; nor do jobs, nor friends, nor beliefs. Our culture encourages us to trade them all in, periodically, on a new model: a new job, a new wife, a new home town. The past is disposable; the future is prefabricated. Nothing lasts forever.

Yet there it was, in black and white, in the official records: Lawrence Gannon and his heirs were granted this land, forever. But it was not to be.

Just six months after Abraham Lincoln was assassinated, as the nation began to bind up its Civil War wounds, Lawrence Gannon died. The year was 1865, and each of his two young sons, John and Christopher, who was my grandfather, inherited half a dream: 80 acres each. But Christopher's life was cut short; in 1890, at the age of 33, he contracted typhoid fever and died, leaving his widow Mary and two babies, including a one-year-old boy named Lawrence Patrick, my father.

I think the saddest family record I own is a folded, yellowed handbill, carefully preserved through the years by my father's sister, Agnes. The handbill reads as follows:

PUBLIC SALE: THE SUBSCRIBER WILL SELL AT AUCTION ON THURSDAY, OCT. 23RD, 1890, AT HER RESIDENCE, 6 MILES SOUTH-EAST OF THE BOROUGH OF BELLE PLAINE, COMMENCING AT 10 O'CLOCK A.M., THE FOLLOWING DESCRIBED PROPERTY:

ONE PAIR OF WORKING HORSES, TWO COLTS, 5 CALVES, FOUR MILCH COWS, ONE 2-YEAR OLD HEIFER, ONE YEARLING BULL, A LOT OF SPRING PIGS, A NEW MCCORMICK BINDER, A NEW TWO-SEATED BUGGY, TWO WAGONS, ONE DRAG, ONE SEEDER, ONE HAY RAKE, ONE CULTIVATOR, ONE CORN PLOW, AND NUMEROUS OTHER ARTICLES.

J B. FITZSIMMONS, AUCTIONEER.

At the bottom of the handbill is the name of Mrs. Chris Gannon, my grandmother.

The old books in the county courthouse record the sale of the Gannon farm for $5,500 to one Joseph Koenig. (The other 80 acres passed out of family hands later.) I was curious what had happened to the old family homestead, so I drove down the dusty gravel road, six miles from the town of Belle Plaine, just as the 1890 handbill advised. I found a mailbox bearing the name Koenig, and drove up the driveway past the green cornfields to a large white farmhouse shaded by old trees

Lawrence Koenig, a husky farmer in his mid-forties, greeted me with some wariness, but his suspicion turned to warm hospitality when I displayed a copy of the deed showing the land passing from my family to his. He welcomed me into his kitchen, where we exchanged family stories. He even brought out a big tin box full of old documents, which apparently passed to his family at the land-sale, including an 1891 court decree of the estate of my grandfather. It showed that he left the grand sum of $684.83 to his widow and two children.

Mr. Koenig, the third generation of his family to farm my great-grandfather's homestead, introduced me to his four sons. He is sure they will carry on for another generation. I wished them well and left, departing with some envy for that land, but with satisfaction that a family has its roots firmly in that soil first tilled by the man from County Meath.

So now, as a third-generation Irish-American, I ponder the irony of our times; sons of the land-hungry immigrants, we find that land ownership is once again an impossible dream for most of us.

Captives of urban living, victims of inflation, hooked on America's culture of mobility, we are land-poor again. Despite this nation's vast open spaces, the land where we must live and work in big urban centers has been divided and subdivided into tiny plots. We are huddled on these plots, with our families and our mortgages. We are not potato-famine poor, but our plastic credit-card wealth is as disconnected from the land as was the evicted Irish tenant farmer.

And that, I think, helps explain why Alex Haley's "Roots" saga struck into our hearts. We are the rootless descendants of immigrants who hungered for America's land and sacrificed mightily to settle it. But we have left the land and crowded together in sprawling cities like so many newly arrived immigrants. This odd reversal of history's tide has left us, I believe, with a void where our sense of roots should be. As Alex Haley dramatically demonstrated, it's easier to understand that void, and to understand yourself, if you can track down your roots. The towns of Trim, Ireland, and Belle Plaine, Minnesota, have proved that to me.

Irish Character:
It's bred in the bone

The Des Moines Sunday Register, March 17, 1985

I don't remember exactly when I discovered I was Irish. The importance of being Irish was not something stressed in my parents' home. They were of the generation that strove to leave immigrant roots behind and join the melting-pot middle class as plain-vanilla Americans. They recalled too vividly the "No Irish Need Apply" mentality of earlier years that treated their parents as second-class citizens.

My father, grandson of a pioneer who traded potato-famine starvation in County Meath, Ireland, for log-cabin subsistence in Scott County, Minnesota, would wear a green tie on

> "What's bred in the bone will out."

St. Patrick's Day, but that was the extent of his proclamation of Irish roots. I don't recall a single party or celebration on any March 17 of my boyhood.

It was only in my father's final years that I prodded from him the information on our ancestors. From a hospital bed, he wrote out what he knew about their immigration, how I would find the town of Trim, whence they came, and where I would find them buried in Belle Plaine, Minn. I went to all those places and began to understand my ancestors, my father and myself.

This process of self-discovery led to formation of one of those central beliefs that govern our lives (if we bother to have any such beliefs). It is the belief in the value of roots and a sense of ethnic identity. It turned my parents' belief on its head: Rejecting melting-pot homogenization, I chose to recognize and celebrate what was bred in bone and blood and to value the differences that I discovered among my fellow Americans. What made the Italians and the

Poles and the Scandinavians and the blacks different from me also made them more interesting, and — once you understand your own ethnic individuality — more understandable.

"What is an ethnic group?" writes Michael Novak, novelist, critic and Slovak-American. "It is a group with historical memory, real or imaginary.....Ethnic memory is not a set of events remembered, but rather a set of instincts, feelings, intimacies, expectations, patterns of emotion and behavior; a sense of reality; a set of stories for individuals – and for people as a whole — to live out."

And so I now live with an ethnic memory and a set of stories to live out. It is a memory of poverty and repression, a story of fierce determination to be independent and self-reliant. It is a memory of land lost and a story of new land reclaimed. It is a memory of people I never knew — peasants grubbing out potatoes on a half-acre of stony soil — who seem nearly as real as the people in my own story — kids with Irish freckles, some with red hair, who watch their father turn St. Patrick's Day into a celebration second only to Christmas.

Now when I read of the Irish mentality, I utter the nervous laugh of self-recognition. "The greatest curse of Ireland has not been English invasions or English misgovernment," writes novelist Sean O'Faolain. "It has been the

A St. Patrick's Day party: Joan and Jim with son Chris and daughters Julie (top right), Beth and Marcy.

exaggeration of Irish virtues — our stubbornness, conservatism, enormous arrogance, our power of resistance, our capacity for taking punishment, our laughter, our endurance; fatalism, devotion to the past, all taken to the point where every human quality can become a vice instead of a virtue."

That one paragraph is a better explanation of the never-ending tragedy of Ulster than any book-length analysis of the political, economic and religious issues. Hold that paragraph up to the face of any honest Irish person you know, and it becomes a mirror,

So if you're lucky enough to share some genuine Irish companionship at a St. Patrick's Day party this weekend, attend with forgiveness. There's an old Irish saying, "What's bred in the bone will out." It means: They can't help it.

The Irish are a people whose wars are always merry and whose songs are always sad. They sing those terribly sad songs, after tipping too many a glass, because there is something in the blood that requires it. St. Patrick's Day is merely the annual public revelation of the very private ethnic memory of the Irish. The memory, as O'Faolain says, "is in the blood and bones of every Irishman, as inflammable as petrol." And he warns: "I suppose that even the most urbane and civil Irishman could, and will if he is wise, acknowledge that there is in him a vestigial angel or devil that, in propitious circumstances, is capable of turning him into a hero or a savage at the memory of what his fathers endured."

They Lived and Died Fighting for the Land

The Des Moines Sunday Register, March 16, 1986

Robert Emmet was one of that seemingly endless line of Irish revolutionary martyrs who wound up on the end of a rope supplied by the King of England. The English had precious little to give to the Irish over the centuries, but there was always rope when the situation called for dispatching another Irishman with foolish ideas of freedom. Emmet reached the end of his particular rope in 1803, following another of those rebellions against English rule that occurred with monotonous regularity and futility over four centuries. He is long gone and mostly forgotten, but there are four places in the world where Emmet is memorialized in statue. His likeness stands in three great cities — Dublin, Washington, DC, and San Francisco — and in a small town in Iowa called Emmetsburg.

The good people of Emmetsburg, founded by a band of Irish immigrants, take their Irish roots seriously. When St. Patrick's Day rolls around, they import goodwill ambassadors from Ireland, dress the town in shamrock green, call out Iowa politicians and send in the clowns for a big parade, dance and banquet. For three days, Emmetsburgers put aside the bleakness of mid-March and the pressures of the farm crisis to escape in an ethnic revelry.

Such rituals are food for the soul, particularly nourishing in times of trouble and in places of merciless winter, and it is in such a time and place that the people of northwest Iowa find themselves. The luck of the Irish, as it is normally conceived, lately has not been with the rural folk of this hard-pressed region; but the truth is, if you cast a long glance over history, that the luck of the Irish is mostly bad, and that's the kind of luck that small-town Iowa struggles against today.

I suppose it is because of my Irish heritage that the festival planners this year have invited me to participate in Emmetsburg's annual celebration. Assuming that I survive the St. Pat's banquet and dance, you will read this as the morning after is unfolding, undoubtedly with regrets.

The festival planners, who throw caution to the wind for this weekend, suggested that I might prepare a few remarks for public consumption at the banquet, and so I retreated to my shelf of Irish literature for inspiration. Irish literature being what it is, I came away mostly depressed and newly angry at the English, but that seemed inappropriate for the occasion.

However, in pondering the grim record of the Irish as peasant farmers, a thought occurred that may be worth sharing, not only with Emmetsburgers, but with people of the land everywhere.

This may be shamelessly sentimental, a mood that seems to overcome me around St. Patrick's Day, but the thought is that what distinguishes the whole of Irish history is the fierceness with which the Irish fought for their land. It was, for the most part, rocky, boggy, unforgiving land on which to eke out a living — but it was theirs, until the English tried to take it.

Irish novelist Sean O'Faolain wrote that Irish peasant farmers "did not prosper. But they held on with a tenacity that is the most moving and astonishing spectacle in the whole Irish story. For these centuries, through generation after generation, starving not by thousands but by millions, falling into the earth like the dung of cattle, weeping and cursing as they slaved, patient alike under the indifference of God and their masters, they clung to their wretched bits of land with a savage fierceness, clung as it were by their bleeding fingernails."

Across Iowa and rural America, farm families ponder the seeming indifference of God and their masters as they try to cling to their threatened land. Their tenacity is to be admired and encouraged. We urban folk who have lost our ancestral attachment to the land sometimes misunderstand that tenacity of the farmer. We forget how much is invested in the soil, not to be measured in ledger books, but to be accounted for in memory, heart, faith and sense of self-worth.

There is a farm in Minnesota that an Irish immigrant named Lawrence Gannon homesteaded when Abe Lincoln was president. It was sold off in 1908

76

after his son Christopher, my grandfather died at, age 33, leaving a penniless widow and two babies. That was my family's "farm crisis."

It is best not to forget, but to cheer those in rural America who cling to what we have lost. For our seeming indifference, we ask forgiveness; for their passionate tenacity, we give thanks.

WE WERE "BOAT PEOPLE" ONCE, TOO

The Des Moines Sunday Register, August 5, 1979

One of the great human tragedies of history occurred in the years 1845 to 1850: the Irish potato famine. The starvation and consequent emigration from Ireland reduced the population of that nation from an estimated 9 million to about 3 million, and cast upon the shores of the world, especially America, a race of destitute people who initially were feared and hated by the native population.

They were the boat people of another age — my boat people. Eventually, they became railroad builders, hod carriers, policemen, politicians, priests, writers, artists and newspapermen. But, for a time, they were despised, discriminated against and feared — feared as low-wage competitors in the labor market and potential burdens on the welfare rolls.

"No Irish need apply" entered the, American idiom because of this influx of an earlier boat people.

> **For my part, I am not yet ready to accept the notion that America has lost its soul.**

America's initial reaction to the horrifying inflow of famine Irish was to tighten immigration regulations. Congress in 1847 passed the Passenger Acts, increasing the cost of ocean passage on U.S. vessels, and port officials in Boston and New York began strictly enforcing rules in a way that turned away many ships loaded with diseased, destitute and dying Irish boat people.

Those rejected vessels went to Canada to

unload their desperate cargo, according to British historian Cecil Woodham-Smith. In her classic study of the Irish famine, "The Great Hunger," she relates how the unwanted ships sailed up the St. Lawrence River to a quarantine station called Grosse Isle.

She writes: "On May 28 (1847), 30 vessels, with 10,000 immigrants on board, were waiting at Grosse Isle; by the 29th, there were 36 vessels, with 13,000 immigrants ... and in all the vessels cases of fever and dysentery had occurred. ... On May 31, 40 vessels were waiting, extending in a line two miles down the St. Lawrence; about 1,100 cases of fever were on Grosse Isle in sheds, tents and laid in rows in the little church; an equal number were on board the ships waiting to be taken off, and a further 45,000 immigrants at least were expected."

They died by the hundreds in the dark, foul holds of those ships; they died by the thousands on that island. They left their homeland because it had become intolerable, and the civilized world didn't want them.

This all has a strikingly familiar ring in 1979, the Year of the Refugee. In Southeast Asia, another of history's human tragedies is unfolding. Tens of thousands of Indochinese, unwilling to live under Communism, are risking their lives in a desperate gamble on the humanitarian instincts of the free world.

They are suffering and dying at sea in overcrowded, leaky boats; they are suffering and dying in island refugee camps, such as Pulau Bidong, the limbo-like waiting station off Malaysia. They have "voted with their feet" against Communism and represent a damning plebescite that should shame their Communist rulers. But the civilized world doesn't know what to do with them.

The United States has responded compassionately, so far. This country took in some 130,000 Indochinese shortly after the fall of the government in South Vietnam, and another 79,000 or so since then. President Carter in June took executive action to double the U.S. quota for such refugees to 14,000 a month; that action would bring in another 168,000 refugees over the next year.

But now the backlash is appearing. The fears and hatreds that met earlier generations of U.S. immigrants are surfacing against the Vietnamese boat people. They will take our jobs, they will go on welfare, they will remind us of an ugly war that took our sons and husbands — so goes the chorus of complaints against the newcomers.

Will the Ugly American please stand up? Yes, if he's asked. That's clear from several polls on attitudes toward the boat people.

The San Francisco Chronicle asked:

"Should the U.S. open its doors to all the Vietnam refugees?" Readers were invited to call in their views. Results: 17,530 callers, or 73 percent, said no, and 6,401 said yes. The highly charged issue drew 17 calls a minute during a 24-hour period, the newspaper reported.

More scientific, nationwide surveys show similar results. The CBS-New York Times poll asked people's views of President Carter's decision to double the Vietnamese-refugee quota; 62 percent disapproved and 34 percent approved. The NBC-Associated Press poll asked: "Do you think the government should allow more Asian refugees to enter the U.S.?" Note that the question did not say "all" the refugees, merely "more." The results: 66 percent said no, 26 percent said yes.

No Vietnamese need apply. Is that the voice of America speaking?

Three weeks ago, President Carter went on television to tell America it was suffering a crisis of the spirit. "It is a crisis that strikes at the very heart and soul and spirit of our national will," he said. "We can see this crisis in the growing doubt about the meaning of our own lives and in the loss of a unity of purpose for our nation."

Carter was not talking about the tragedy of the refugees and American attitudes toward saving them, but just take his message and play it against what those polls say.

"We have always believed that we were part of a great movement of humanity called democracy, involved in the search for freedom. And that belief has always strengthened us in our purpose. But just as we are losing our confidence in the future, we are also beginning to close the door on our past. In a nation that was proud of hard work, strong families, close-knit communities and our faith in God, too many of us now tend to worship self-indulgence and consumption."

For my part, I am not yet ready to accept the notion that America has lost its soul. But I think the plight of the boat people provides a clear-cut test of whether this generation of Americans, descendants of boat people, still believe in the meaning of this country's past and has faith in the future of the

American dream.

The boat people are, above all, "involved in the search for freedom." Saving them from their tragedy will involve snaring our wealth, our jobs, our welfare funds, our neighborhoods. But if America is not the haven for the hopeless of this world, there is none.

"Give me your tired, your poor, your huddled masses yearning to breathe free, the wretched refuse of your teeming shore. ..." That is the inscription on the Statue of Liberty. It does not say: "Give me your strong, your rich, your taxpaying single individuals who will never go on welfare, your best and your brightest." If that is what America wants to say now, we should tear down the Statue of Liberty and put up a Brain Drain Beacon with the inscription: No Vietnamese Need Apply.

My ancestors were on those potato-famine boats. My children will inherit the America we are shaping today. It will be immensely saddening if their America loses its unique identity as the open shore of freedom.

THE MAGIC OF IRELAND, WHERE BUILDINGS TALK

The Des Moines Sunday Register, October 31, 1982

Ireland is a magic place, the sort of place where it is entirely possible to have a conversation with the ruins of a 600-year-old building. To talk to the building, if you want it to talk back, you must stand at the appointed place. The place is a specific spot in the town of Trim, in County Meath, which not so incidentally is where a man named Lawrence Gannon grew up before he left for America around 1850. He was my great-grandfather.

The place is called the Echo Gate. It is nothing more than a stone gate at the entry to a broad, green meadow bordering the River Boyne. Across the river, perhaps a quarter-mile away from the gate, are the ruins of a medieval monastery, one of several ancient architectural relics that grace the little town, where so much history is written in stone.

> We laughed at being mistaken for a married couple — or perhaps, an unmarried couple — by innkeepers and restaurant waitresses.

I am standing at the Echo Gate, in the fading twilight of a chill December afternoon, with a young, freckled, red-haired woman, who looks as Irish as anyone you can find in this country. But she has never been to Ireland before, and she has never talked to buildings that talk back. She is my daughter Julie, now 20, and at this moment not quite certain whether to humor her father or hide in the car while he makes a fool of himself.

We peer across the river to the distant monastery, both wondering how the building could talk back from so far away. But we are told that it will, so I begin shouting.

"Hello."

Pause.

"Hello."

We laugh.

"I can hear you."

Pause.

"I can hear you."

I shout, and the building shouts back. Julie shouts, and it responds. Through some quirk of physics, it has been doing this for centuries. There is a strange sensation that you are shouting across the centuries, to the time before your known ancestors, and hearing back from an unknown realm.

It would be easy to become superstitious in Ireland. The Irish are, of course. Across the river, on the monastery grounds, there is an old cemetery. Before trying the Echo Gate, Julie and I had explored the ruins and the grave-yard, locating what a local guidebook called the "Tomb of the Jealous Man and Woman." The raised tomb of Sir Lucas Dillon and his Lady Jane features effigies of the couple dressed in Elizabethan costume, sculpted in stone — lying side by side in death, with a massive sword stretched out between them. If you look closely, in the hollows of the sculpture, you will find a curious collection of straight pins — the kind you put in a pin cushion. Some of them are rusty, as if they had been here some time, while others are shiny, as if left just yesterday. "Pins in the top of the tomb," the guide book advises, "are left there by persons who come here to seek a cure for warts."

That's Ireland. A place to talk to buildings, and have them talk back. A place to seek to shed your warts on an ancient tomb. A place where you can rent a room for the night for $10, and be given a hot-water bottle to sleep with, because the house is unheated and you can see your breath in the bedroom. This is definitely not Disneyland. But it is an experience, one that Julie and I will not forget.

We spent a week together in Ireland. We bought Christmas presents in Dublin's jewelry stores and woolen shops, drank Irish ale in many pubs, drove down quiet country lanes in the rain, sat around warm fires drinking tea with the friendly old people who rent out bed-and-breakfast accommodations, and ate long, relaxed meals in uncrowded restaurants, where we talked of the past

— mine — and the future — hers.

We laughed at being mistaken for a married couple — or perhaps, an unmarried couple — by innkeepers and restaurant waitresses. The notion flattered us both, I thought. We walked on a deserted beach along the Irish Sea near Arklow, gathering sea-shells, and we listened to the deep-throated foghorns booming out into the darkness at Dun Laoghaire harbor. We ate big Irish breakfasts of eggs and bacon and toast and tea, and read Irish newspapers with front-page headlines over stories about Ted Kennedy's quitting the presidential race back home.

Best of all, we stored away the memory of a shared experience. Some day, in some December twilight, the memory will echo across the river of a lifetime, like some crazy building that talks, and I will smile.

Searching for my Confederate ancestor

Gannett News Service, February 5, 1995

NEW ORLEANS — Considering that he had been dead for nearly 78 years, it wasn't all that hard to find Private Dennis Cavanaugh.

He had left a fairly good paper trail. It led from an antique steamer trunk to the National Archives, to a Civil War historian in Baton Rouge, Louisiana, to Tulane University's library and finally to Greenwood Cemetery here in the city where he landed as a teenage Irish immigrant. Young Dennis, out of County Galway, arrived on that tide of impoverished Irish that flooded America's shores in the 1850s after Ireland's potato famine. His older brother Patrick, my great-grandfather, had come to New Orleans in 1852, and had sent money home to bring Dennis over to join him in the promised land of America.

Dennis arrived to find the Promised Land breaking in two and heading for war. I've always wondered what a poor, young country boy, just arrived in a big city frothing with talk of secession and war, would have thought about it all. Having just escaped serfdom he would not have held much stock in slavery. Having never known a Negro before, he probably knew or cared little about them. He couldn't have understood or much cared about the causes and the stakes of the war.

His brother Patrick took a steamboat up the Mississippi River to homestead on the Minnesota prairie, but Dennis stayed in New

> We had a nice visit. I sat on the tomb next to his and ate my brown-bag lunch.

Orleans as Louisiana seceded from the Union and the guns began to roar. Soon he was Private Dennis Cavanaugh, CSA.

My search for Dennis began some years ago with the discovery of a small box of old letters in a trunk that once belonged to my grandmother. One letter was from a nurse at Camp Nicholls, a Confederate old-soldiers' home, to my Aunt Agnes in Minnesota, who must have been trying to contact Dennis. It said that he had been "very sick" and was unable to write, but now he was "on the road to recovery." That turned out to be a dead end road for the old soldier; he died three days after the nurse wrote, on February 27, 1917.

That sad old letter raised questions I wanted to answer. I wanted to know what had happened to Dennis in the war, why he had wound up in the Confederate soldiers' home, and where he had been buried. I am not sure why this was important to me, except as a link to my past and an understanding of a piece of history that shaped my family.

The Civil War divided my great-grandfather from his brother. It was a north-south split among my ancestors that mirrored what had happened to the country. It was a classic example of how history shapes lives. I have my roots in Minnesota partly because my great-grandfather wanted no part of that war, while his younger brother, perhaps seeking adventure or glory or just a meal-ticket, enlisted to fight for the South.

I have some of the answers now. Records at the National Archives in Washington show that 18-year-old Dennis enlisted April 3,1862, as New Orleans was about to fall to Union forces. He fought with Miles' Louisiana Legion until being captured June 7, 1863, at Port Hudson, Louisiana, a Confederate fort on the Mississippi River. He spent months in a federal prison near Richmond before being paroled, and then was assigned to fight again with the 1st Louisiana Heavy Artillery Regiment. At the war's end, he returned to New Orleans.

Civil War historian Arthur Bergeron Jr. led me to the papers of the old soldiers' home in Tulane's library. They showed that Dennis had spent nearly 19 years of his life, from 1898 to his death, with his old comrades-in-arms at the home. They also led me to Greenwood Cemetery. In New Orleans, the dead aren't buried. They are entombed above ground, due to the high water table in this city built on alluvial muck. On a sunny day, I walked alone in this city of the dead, looking for the Soldier's Home Tomb. When I found it — a stone building carved with Civil War cannon on its sides, I knew I had found Dennis.

I probably was his first visitor in decades, perhaps since the day he was buried. We had a nice visit. I sat on the tomb next to his and ate my brown-bag lunch. There was a tiny sprig of green growing in the crack between two of the 40 numbered vaults where Dennis lies with his Civil War comrades. It wasn't, but I fancied it to be a shamrock. Dennis would have been astonished that his brother's great-grandson came to find him, after all these decades. Sure and he would have been pleased entirely.

4

TRAINS

"Sometimes I'd go with him on the Milwaukee Road. We'd eat in dining cars, with silver, linen tablecloths and polite black waiters. We'd sleep in Pullman cars — an experience so sweet for a small boy that it lives in memory with a special brilliance — and in the morning we'd wake to see South Dakota rushing by."

DEATH OF THE MILWAUKEE ROAD, THE RAILROAD THAT TOUCHED MY LIFE

The Des Moines Sunday Register, April 29, 1979

It is sad to see a part of America, and a part of your own past, dying a slow and humiliating death. You wonder how something so big and powerful as a huge railroad, built of steel and machinery and muscle and pride could be slipping so feebly, so faintly, into its grave. You'd expect a great roar, a piercing hiss of steam, a tremendous protest by the thousands of people whose lives have been touched by the giant. Instead, there is a gathering in court, a premature probate of the dying giant's will.

The Milwaukee Road is dying. That is what the stories emerging from the bankruptcy court in Chicago really mean. Oh, maybe some truncated remnant of the Chicago, Milwaukee, St. Paul & Pacific Railroad will survive the bankruptcy proceedings. But it would be only a pale shadow of the proud line that spanned two-thirds of the continent, from Louisville to Seattle.

It wouldn't be my railroad, the old Milwaukee Road. It's not my railroad, of course. I don't own one share of stock in it, never worked for it, never sold it a nickel's worth of anything. But it's my railroad in the sense that it has touched my life and my memory in the personal ways that railroads touch people's lives.

That's the funny thing about railroads. They aren't like other businesses. Why are there so many folk songs about railroads? They don't

> I went out and bought a Milwaukee Road passenger train set made by Lionel. It runs under the Christmas tree each year.

write folk songs about insurance companies or the plastics industry. They write folk songs about railroads because people love railroads, because railroads reach into people's lives and make a difference.

The railroads crossed the prairies and the mountains and created new towns. They employed generations of men in the building, and more generations in running and maintaining the trains, They made many men rich and famous, and they ruined others. They crossed the backyards of America, separated the swell parts of town from the wrong-side-of-the-tracks, generated romantic literature and song, and blew their lonesome whistles into the tape recorders of our minds.

The Milwaukee Road was the one that touched my life. When I was growing up in Minneapolis, it was a part of my boyhood. My dad was a grain merchant who rode trains, especially Milwaukee trains, almost as often as the conductors did.

The Milwaukee Road station, a grand old building with a huge clock tower, was a couple of blocks from his office at the Minneapolis Grain Exchange. I remember meeting his trains there, overwhelmed and overjoyed at the sight and sound of the hissing steam engines — and later, the throaty, throbbing diesel streamliners.

Dad would be returning from calling on elevator operators in towns like Ipswich and Sisseton, S.D., and Buffalo Lake, Minn. To a boy, it seemed a romantic way to make a living, riding the railroad; but it probably was drudgery.

Sometimes I'd go with him on the Milwaukee Road. We'd eat in dining cars, with silver, linen tablecloths and polite black waiters. We'd sleep in Pullman cars — an experience so sweet for a small boy that it lives in memory with a special brilliance — and in the morning we'd wake to see South Dakota rushing by.

There was a memorable trip to South Dakota to see the ranch my dad and his business partner had bought. The ranch was near McLaughlin, a town too small to merit a stop by the fast "Olympian Hiawatha" train from Chicago to Seattle.

Such considerations did not deter my father, a man of iron will and great capacity to browbeat. He somehow scared some poor ticket agent into selling us two tickets to McLaughlin, even though the train never stopped there. And then he managed to browbeat a harried conductor into stopping the train at

McLaughlin, against all the rules, because he had two tickets that said he was going from Minneapolis to McLaughlin. I remember getting off the train in McLaughlin and thinking my dad could accomplish anything he set his mind to.

My dad, Lawrence P. Gannon, on his horse "Sargeant," at his KG Ranch in South Dakota.

The Milwaukee Road cut right through that ranch of his, and you could stand on a hill and look down at the track, and hear those steam whistles coming from miles away. The long freights would have two huge steam engines working in tandem, struggling upgrade and churning out magnificent plumes of black smoke. It's a mental snapshot that will never die, no matter what the bankruptcy court decides.

When I was older, I'd ride the Milwaukee Road between Minneapolis and Milwaukee, where I went to college. By then, the trains were getting older, slower and less reliable, but it was fun anyway.

Later, the distinctive orange-and-maroon passenger trains, which once made the 400-mile run from Chicago to St. Paul in less than 400 minutes, disappeared entirely. And now the rest of the old Milwaukee Road is disappearing. You could see it coming, though.

A few years ago, in one of those fits of nostalgia that drive fathers to do things that must puzzle their sons, I went out and bought a Milwaukee Road passenger train set made by Lionel. It runs under the Christmas tree each year, and is carefully stored in its boxes the rest of the time. My kids think it is a toy. They do not understand.

Someday, I am going to write a folk song about the Milwaukee Road. It ought to be remembered.

QUIET THOUGHTS RIDE ON THE NIGHT TRAIN

The Des Moines Sunday Register, July 5, 1981

Across the vast openness that is named Montana a train called "The Empire Builder" glides through the twilight. It is a long — and some would say boring — ride, but the passing of the hours and the miles prompts a quiet musing, a traveler's reverie.

The thinking starts with a plain-faced fact that is so easily forgotten in our world of rush and congestion: The American prairie is still out there, rolling unbroken to the horizon, still largely unspoiled and undeveloped. It is so huge, so nearly empty, so almost still a frontier, that the scattered markings of 20th-century civilization seem barely noticeable. This is not a land that has been chewed up, spat out and left useless.

> You can easily imagine a band of Cheyenne Indians on horseback suddenly appearing on the ridge of a bluff in the distance.

Herds of Angus and Hereford cows, with their tag-along spring calves by their sides, graze in the setting sun, casting long shadows as the train rolls by. Cattle are everywhere, but people are few. Abandoned homes built by the sides of wandering streams mark where some hardy souls once lived, but now the people are mostly clustered in towns most of the train-riders have never heard of. Wolf Point and Saco, Malta and Harlem, Havre and Glasgow — they slide by the train's windows with quick images of grain elevators, hardware stores, bars with Grain Belt beer signs. What is happening on a Tuesday night in Malta,

Montana? The world does not know, or much care.

The West is different. That is a thought that occurs as this train rolls on and on, through the emptiness of the range. The people here, and their view of the world, must be different — shaped by the isolation and distance from their fellow countrymen. Their concerns, their expectations, their aspirations are not likely to be the same as those of people in Boston, Cleveland or Des Moines. They are separated from the rest of the country — the country that they see on television news in the evening and that they read about in newspapers and magazines — by great physical distances and, it seems probable, by a huge psychological gap. How could someone out here understand, or care about, the lives of welfare mothers in urban slums or the pressures of living on the fast-track society in New York or Washington?

The author, then about age 10, flanked by his dad (left) and a ranch hand on the KG Ranch, with the main line of The Milwaukee Road cutting across the background.

Montana still looks like the background in the paintings of Charles M. Russell, its famous cowboy artist. You can easily imagine a band of Cheyenne Indians on horseback suddenly appearing on the ridge of a bluff in the distance. The past does not seem so distant here; the frontier was just yesterday.

And perhaps the frontier is tomorrow as well. This is not dying region, but one discovering new life. The resources of the future lie under the prairie.

The oil wells of the Williston Basin are pumping along the tracks of the old Great Northern Railroad as the "Empire Builder" hurries into the night. Passing through Tioga, North Dakota, suggests scene from Texas — or perhaps Saudi Arabia. Long lines of rail tank cars wait on side tracks outside a refinery, where a flame-topped tower is flaring — that is wasting — unwanted natural gas.

Flat cars on sidings along this route give testimony to another giant energy project under way — a gas pipeline across the plains. The cars each hold nine huge sections steel pipe, each 48 inches in diameter, for a gas line running hundreds of miles across Montana and the Dakotas to Iowa. The nation is becoming increasingly dependent on this seemingly empty quarter to maintain its energy-intensive economy. The coal, oil, gas and electricity that Midwesterners burn in the future will be imported from the West. But we are much better off being dependent on Montana than Arabia.

You begin to understand the frustration of the West. It offers much to the nation, but has little political clout. The "Sagebrush Rebellion" against Washington that has spread through these arid highlands of the American Outback reflects the West's restiveness. The people who have run the government in recent years generally have not understood the West. Jimmy Carter, from the swampy Deep South, never appreciated the importance of water as a political issue, and badly bungled policies important to Westerners. Westerners feel they are in better hands with Ronald Reagan. He may be Hollywood, but he can enjoy riding a horse or fixing a fence or being alone on his ranch. That's Western.

The train whistles its way through the North Dakota night, highballing towards St. Paul, Minnesota, where a century ago a man named James J. Hill had a vision of a single rail line running from the Minnesota capital to Seattle — a Northwest Passage to the Pacific Coast. Hill, the original "empire builder," pushed his Great Northern Railroad across these prairies, over the Rocky Mountains and to the Pacific in only a few years, in an age when the West was not only a vast, unconquered empire, but a metaphor for unlimited possibilities.

Hill is gone now, and so is his Great Northern, absorbed into the giant Burlington Northern system. One train named after him — one train running on a government subsidy that might anytime disappear — still rumbles on through the Western night.

You cannot put an economic value on something so metaphysical, but it is worth something to ride that train today to develop some appreciation for the history of this Western expanse and the promise it still holds. The train still touches this land, and the land reaches out with its images to set the mind a-musing. You'll never feel it inside a jet at 35,000 feet, but the American West retains a kind of lonesome allure that penetrates the quiet darkness of the night train.

COMBINING MY PASSIONS:
A TRAIN, COUNTRY MUSIC AND
500 CLOSE FRIENDS

The Des Moines Sunday Register, September 1, 1985

Country singer Johnny Cash once recorded a song titled "I have a thing about trains." It's a nostalgic lament over the decline of the passenger train in the jet age.

Cash's song expresses one of my own quirks: I have a thing about trains, too. I also have a thing about country music; I'd drop just about anything to watch Willie Nelson or Waylon Jennings or Johnny Cash perform.

And a third thing of mine — as long as I'm baring my bib-overall soul here — is a love for farms and farmers. The land and the people who toil upon it are the bedrock of Iowa.

> **And thus is born an idea composed of nostalgia, symbolism, rural roots and just a touch of insanity.**

When a rare opportunity comes along to put these three elements together, I can't let it pass. And thus is born an idea composed of nostalgia, symbolism, rural roots and just a touch of insanity. The idea: First, get a passenger train. Then get 500 tickets to the Farm Aid country-music concert planned for Sunday, September 22, in Champaign, Illinois, a 12-hour extravaganza featuring everyone who's anyone in country and western music.

Finally, gather 500 people who really care about what's happening on the farm — farmers, rural bankers, farm suppliers, agribusiness people, and others — and take them on that train to Champaign.

It would be a whistle-stop tour across Iowa, bringing together the people who in reality are all on a train called American agriculture — the train that feeds us all, the train that now needs all help and recognition it can get.

Crazy? Maybe. But this once-in-a-lifetime ride is worth doing — just for the fun of it. And actually there's more than fun involved. Symbols are important, and if this train could symbolize the unity and good will among Iowans that's needed to ease our farmers' problems, then it would make a statement worth making.

And so we're going to do it. The train will be The Register's Farm Aid Express. Thanks to the Chicago & North Western Railroad, it will highball across Iowa on Saturday, September 21, Carroll to Clinton, picking up farmers, friends of farmers and lovers of country music. The train will rumble through Jefferson, Boone, Ames, Nevada, Marshalltown, Tama, Belle Plaine, Cedar Rapids. Clinton and other points on the North Western mainline. We hope to find kindred spirits in all those communities to join us, and others to cheer them on at pro-farmer rallies at trackside.

We'll invite farm organizations, agribusinesses and banks to send people.

The crowd awaits the "All aboard!" at the start of the Farm Aid Express run at Carroll, Iowa.

And we'll invite others who ought to care about aiding farmers — Governor Terry Branstad, Senators Charles Grassley and Tom Harkin, Iowa's six congressmen, U.S. Agriculture Secretary John Block, and Iowa's ag secretary, Bob Lounsberry.

You can't solve the farm problem by riding a train or singing country songs. But it can't hurt, and it might help, to get all those people together, in a good mood, and get better acquainted. We might learn something about each other and the other guy's problems — whether the other guy is the farmer, the banker or the politician. At least, we can have a good time.

Our train will chug into Chicago and head south for Champaign, arriving Saturday evening. On Sunday, it's hoe-down time: Willie Nelson, Waylon Jennings, Merle Haggard, Alabama, Kenny Rogers, Loretta Lynn, Bob Dylan, Charlie Pride (and a few urban interlopers, including the Beach Boys) will perform in the University of Illinois football stadium.

The idea, says Willie Nelson, who proposed the concert, is "to call attention to the problems of the American farmer and see what can be done about them". The event is supposed to raise money to help needy farmers, though the exact use of the money hasn't been explained.

Some people are worried about where the money will go. Frankly, I doubt a concert can raise enough money to solve the farm problem in Clarke County, much less in America — but that's not the point. It will attract immense attention, just as the recent Live Aid rock concert riveted world attention on starvation in Ethiopia.

Wouldn't it be a shame if they held a Farm Aid concert and no farmers came? Shouldn't Iowa, the heartland of American Agriculture, be seen and heard there? I think so. But then, I have this thing about trains.

A RIDE ON THE FARM AID EXPRESS

The Des Moines Sunday Register, September 22, 1985

ABOARD THE FARM AID EXPRESS - The dampened fields of corn and soybeans whiz by at 70 mph as 13-year-old Brian Knapp wows the riders of this train with hard-driving country rock hammered from his trusty guitar.

"There's a whole lotta shakin' goin' on," Brian wails as the small knot of travelers surrounding him claps hands and hoots approval. Bill Gannon, the John Deere dealer from Mingo, and John Chrystal, Des Moines' own country banker, watch Brian's imitation of Jerry Lee Lewis with an appreciation evident in wide smiles and toe-tapping.

Indeed, as The Register's Farm Aid Express highballs down the line — at this moment just a few miles east of the muddy Mississippi — there is indeed a whole lot of shakin' goin' on. The Chicago and North Western railway special is shaking, rattling and rolling through a drizzly afternoon on its 12-hour pilgrimage to Sunday's Farm Aid concert in Champaign, Illinois.

As this is written, I am sitting at the back of the dome car, trying to sort out the thoughts and feelings that ride along these rails with 500 Iowa farm people who are joined in something that few of us will ever forget. What began as a lark is

> There, standing in a familiar pose, was a couple who did a living re-creation of Grant Wood's classic painting, American Gothic, complete right down to the same dress and a five-tine pitchfork.

evolving into something much more memorable than we had a right to expect.

This railroad crusade to Farm Aid ignited a spark of enthusiasm wherever it stopped. It howled into Carroll about 8 a.m. in a full-throated roar of its three engines and blaring whistle — a spine-tingling hello and welcome to a big crowd whose spirits were undampened by the morning rain. It was the same at every stop — Boone, Ames, Marshalltown, Cedar Rapids and Clinton — big crowds, banners, balloons, speeches, and presentations of everything from keys to the city to a bushel basket of fresh garden vegetables.

As impressive as these organized rallies were, what struck an even more poignant note were the spontaneous, individual tributes that we witnessed all along the line across the state.

Farm families in pickup trucks parked at the country-road crossings to catch a glimpse of the Farm Aid Express. They waved at the speeding train, snapped pictures, smiled and cheered. They parked to watch the train glide over the Kate Shelley high bridge west of Boone, and townsfolk in the hamlets between stops gathered at trackside to witness the passing.

Engineer Jim with son Michael, son-in-law Tom Shoop, and daughters Julie and Beth at the train's stop in Ames, Iowa.

Young Mesquakie children smiled and waved as we highballed through the Tama Indian settlement, where several residents climbed atop a roof to get a better vantage point for viewing. Somewhere west of Cedar Rapids, train riders witnessed a sight that must have made some blink — there, standing in a familiar pose, was a couple who did a living re-creation of Grant Wood's classic painting, American Gothic, complete right down to the same dress and a five-tine pitchfork.

I don't know why they all were there, but I read their enthusiastic greetings as a message of kinship to the riders of this train. They seemed to be saying "We are with you" and their presence had more meaning to us than they could have known.

On board, you could find a mix of moods that ran the gamut from serious debate of farm-policy problems to loud-voiced high-jinks. The two snack-bar cars were jammed like a singles bar on a Saturday night, dispensing drinks and lunches. At the rear of the train, two fancy business cars and a plush dome car provided a private retreat for a privileged few, including Governor Terry Branstad and Tennessee's former Senator Howard Baker, a presidential aspirant who found it worth his while to spend six hours in Iowa on a train, politicking and snapping pictures.

You couldn't sit in the rear observation car, with its plush blue carpet, velvet chairs and backdoor speaking platform, without feeling like Harry Truman in 1948, when he whistle- stopped across Iowa. And you couldn't sit in the cab of the lead engine — as I did between Boone and Ames — without resurrecting those childhood dreams of being railroad engineer. Some fantasies come true, for a fleeting moment, at least.

It will be weeks if not months before we know whether any of this has any meaning beyond fond memories. But as we speed across the Illinois prairie, past cornfields and farmhouses, there is a strong feeling in this quiet corner of the dome car that it was worth doing.

5

POLITICS

"Reagan had all the right lyrics in 1980 and mobilized the country-music vote into an electoral landslide. If you look at a map of the 1980 election returns, you'll find that Reagan's margins were biggest in places where country music is strongest. He was as popular as Waylon Jennings in the West, most of the South and non-urban areas in the North. Jimmy Carter, who got his campaign off to a good start by having Willie Nelson sing the national anthem at his nominating convention, lost touch with jukebox America and wound up carrying states like Rhode Island and Hawaii, where mommas don't let their babies grow up to be cowboys."

OUR MAN SURVIVES
THE GREAT DEBATE

The Wall Street Journal, September 27, 1976

Philadelphia — "I'm just glad the first question wasn't on adultery," Jimmy Carter said. The smiling Democratic nominee was shaking the hand of ABC newsman Frank Reynolds, just after finishing his first televised debate with President Ford.

"I appreciated that, too," drawled Rosalynn Carter, who was standing at her husband's side now on the stage of the old Walnut Street Theater here. Mr. Carter's remarks about adultery in a Playboy interview had dominated campaign discussion in the previous few days, and the Carters clearly were relieved not only that the debate was over but also that adultery hadn't come up.

> I had spent almost a week alternating between euphoria over being selected for this important task and stark terror at the possibility of bungling it.

Actually, everyone involved was relieved after the weird ending to this first debate between presidential candidates in 16 years — and after the biggest broadcasting foul-up of all time. Everyone, that is, except ABC producer Elliot Bernstein, the man responsible for seeing that the program went off without a hitch. He was outside in a television trailer, so distraught over the 27-minute loss of the program's sound that his co-workers reportedly warned others not to go near him.

I was certainly relieved, despite the electronic snafu, because the end of the debate last Thursday night also marked the end of six days of dreadful tenseness for me. As one of the three journalists on the questioning panel, I had spent almost a week alternating between euphoria over being selected for this important task and stark terror at the possibility of bungling it.

But in those tension-shedding moments just after the event, it was obvious that we all had survived — the panelists, the debate's sponsors from the League of Women Voters, and the candidates. There would be two more debates, and the campaigns would go on pretty much as before. But a piece of history had happened, and I was lucky enough to get an insider's look at it. What follows are some glimpses and impressions of the event from my perspective.

The announcement last Monday that the league had selected Mr. Reynolds of ABC, Elizabeth Drew of the New Yorker magazine, and me to be the three panelists had started things happening to each of us. Suddenly we were the tar-

The Ford-Carter debate panel awaits the debaters. From left: Frank Reynolds of ABC, the author, Elizabeth Drew of The New Yorker magazine, and moderator Edwin Newman of NBC.

gets of every special interest group, ordinary citizen and kook who wanted to plant a question for President Ford or Mr. Carter.

The phone calls and wires poured in. Callers were told politely that I wasn't available, but some left their questions with my office. The National Gay Task Force wanted a question asked on homosexuals' rights. The American Bakers Association had an irritated query on Mr. Ford's recent decision to raise the tariff on imported sugar. A friend in Green Bay, Wisconsin, suggested asking about "genetic engineering." A wire from Fort Worth, Texas, tried to plant a query on "how much 1975 peanut subsidy did Carter receive." A telegram delivered to the theater just before the debate proposed this zinger: "How soon do you think it will take for a complete Soviet take-over of the U.S.?"

The panelists had decided that we would prepare our own questions independently, without any consultation or coordination. We also agreed to keep our mouths shut before the debate, and so for the first time in my life I was in the awkward position of refusing calls from reporters and dodging my own friends and colleagues.

I collected a stack of news articles, speeches and position papers of the two candidates and began reviewing their stands on issues. Then I prepared a list of 12 questions (I only asked four of them) on topics that seemed to me to be of concern to voters: inflation, education, housing, unemployment. Because of my own journalistic background, my questions dealt mostly with economic issues.

In early afternoon of the debate day, panelists and moderator Edwin Newman of NBC joined two stand-ins for Mr. Ford and Mr. Carter for a dry run. Its purpose is richly ironic now: to test the sound system.

"President Ford" was John Kostic, a truck salesman from Wilmington, Delaware, who is strong-voiced, husky, and six-feet, one-inch tall, just like Mr. Ford. "Jimmy Carter" was Bob Salica, a student at Temple University here, who, clad in a Levi denim suit, is soft-spoken and stands 5 feet, 9 inches, just like the former Georgia governor. The dry run went like this:

Question from Mr. Reynolds: "What is your position on your position on your position?"

Jimmy Carter: "My position on that is that I have a position, and I have researched that position."

Rebuttal from President Ford: "My position on that position is the opposite of his position."

During this necessary nonsense, a tiny problem became clear: Although the television and radio sound worked fine and the theater audience could hear a public-address system in the seats, the panelists and moderator 15 feet from the candidates couldn't hear the answers clearly unless the candidates shouted. "We've got a serious problem here," said producer Bernstein, who ordered a loudspeaker rigged up behind the panelists. A second dry run, conducted later that afternoon, made everyone think that all the sound problems had been solved.

At 8 p.m. Thursday, we gathered in the lobby of the Ben Franklin Hotel for the one-block walk to the theater. The street was barricaded, lined with police, and dotted with horse manure — testimony to the daylong presence of the mounted cops. As we picked our way down the empty street, bathed in eerie TV light, between long rows of police, I couldn't help feeling I was being marched to a public hanging,

Waiting in a dressing room, we groped for comic relief. "Maybe Gene McCarthy's suit will come through and spare us," Liz Drew said. But no judicial reprieve arrived.

Inside the theater, the audience of league guests and journalists was being told to keep quiet throughout the debate. Ed Newman was double-checking the little electronic boxes labeled "Mr. Ford" and "Mr. Carter," at his left hand. Each had three tiny lights to flash when the speaker had one minute or 30 seconds or no time remaining for his answer. A professional debate timer sat offstage controlling these boxes and similar devices mounted on the TV cameras facing the candidates.

The water glasses that had been standing on the podiums in the afternoon had disappeared, as had the ringlike devices around them that had been designed to prevent spill. Now the water was safely hidden on a shelf in each speaker's stand. Another risk had been further reduced by the candidates' cautious TV advisers.

The candidates arrived only a couple of minutes before starting time, 9:30 p.m. They exchanged a quick greeting, shook hands, and took their battle stations.

President Ford appeared calm, almost stoic. He seemed an imposing figure, his height and strong shoulders giving him a commanding presence. His big hands firmly gripped the rimlike top of the semicircular podium. He looked as though he could lift it over his head and throw it at me.

Mr. Carter, in contrast, looked surprisingly small, frail and vulnerable. He seemed extremely nervous (something he publicly admitted later) and began to sweat heavily, the droplets evident on his brow and chin. Physically, it seemed an unfair match-up.

"Stand by, 10 seconds'" somebody offstage shouted. Then came the sound of a dog barking (perhaps a canine bomb-sniffer?). Frank Reynolds, a polished television professional, was clearing his throat over and over, preparing to ask the first questions. I couldn't be sure, but it seemed that Mr. Carter was saying a short prayer; his hands were folded for a moment, and his head was bowed.

In his introduction, moderator Newman reminded us that the TV audience might reach 100 million in the U.S. and millions more abroad — a reminder that hardly put us at ease. Soon, Mr. Reynolds asked the first question, about unemployment, and the debate was on.

Mr. Carter responded with a blizzard of words, arranged in long, convoluted sentences and spoken in a rapid Georgia drawl. It might have been my nervousness, but I couldn't grasp any meaning from this verbal torrent. That made me even more nervous.

Soon it was my turn, and after I managed to get out a question, I relaxed. Before long, everyone seemed more relaxed, particularly Mr. Carter. His answers became more forceful. At first afraid to be aggressive because he didn't want to be disrespectful to a President, the Democrat dropped his reticence after Mr. Ford showed that the President, on this occasion, was just another politician.

The debate settled into a comfortable routine that rapidly consumed the time. Then, nine minutes before the scheduled finish, the audio crisis hit. Mr. Carter was speaking of "a breakdown in the trust" of Americans in the FBI and other intelligence agencies when there was an electronic breakdown somewhere (later traced to a tiny, $1 audio part).

Mr. Newman informed the candidates that the sound was off, and for the first time, the

> He [President Ford] looked as though he could lift the podium over his head and throw it at me.

audience broke into laughter and talk. "I hope you'll grant clemency to whoever pulled the plug," Mr. Reynolds said to the President, who shook his head in disgust. Mr. Carter, grinning broadly, chimed in: "Mr. Kelley (head of the FBI) may not have liked what I was saying."

The audience was getting noisier and broke into applause when Mr. Carter sat down. At 11:06, the candidates were told that the cameras would be taken off them to allow them to wipe their brows: each mopped his head with a handkerchief.

The most interesting aspect of this awkward period was the candidates' behavior toward each other. The two men didn't exchange a word, and they hardly even exchanged a glance. No small talk, no smiles, no recognition. These two men, who never have to wait for a bus, or wait in line at a bank or wait for anything, spent 27 minutes waiting in silence while Mr. Newman kept counting off numbers. "Testing, one, two, three, four, five, this is Edwin Newman at the Walnut Street Theater in Philadelphia."

At 11:18, the sound was restored, but the flow of the debate — and the momentum Mr. Carter seemed to be gathering — was lost. He ran through his closing statement, a rehash of his basic campaign speech, and finished in a voice barely audible to me. Mr. Ford's closing statement was stiff, wooden, spoken without much feeling. As the President finished, Mr. Carter's face appeared tired, sad, disappointed. He knew what he conceded later: that he hadn't won but at best had only managed a draw. Mr. Ford looked pleased.

Finally, at 11:27, Mr. Newman said, "Good night." Then it was over, and I knew I would never forget it.

Hubert Humphrey, Free at Last

The Wall Street Journal, February 2, 1977

WASHINGTON - With a bittersweet mixture of sadness and hope, the Senate is witnessing the last race of that perennial runner, Hubert Humphrey. This time, he's running for his life.

The sadness swells from the shocking appearance of the famous Minnesota Senator. Cancer surgery and chemotherapy treatments have reduced him to a scary-looking shadow of himself. His suit drapes loosely about his thinned frame. His once-cherubic face has a chiseled, angular look that suggests a sinking-in. Only a thin fringe of hair remains, turned dusty-white. His appearance literally stops passers-by, prompting an anguished second look.

But the hope springs from seeing how this aging lion devours the gloom in others' eyes. He smothers sadness with his outpouring of good cheer, unstoppable determination, genuine humor and total lack of self-pity. Strong of voice, animated in Senate debate, active in cranking out yet another batch of Humphrey-style solutions to the nation's problems, the "Happy Warrior" is exorcising despair with the politics of hope and his zest for life.

In so doing, this most famous of all liberal Democrats may be carving out for himself a special role in Jimmy Carter's Washington. His long dream of becoming President, and his brief hope of becoming Senate majority leader, are behind him forever. The reins of power have eluded his grasp, but a unique position of influence has not. He aims to become the liberal conscience of Washington: prodding the cautious Carterites to do more than they dare, challenging the Congress to be active and innovative, not just responsive to the White House lead.

Only a month ago, it seemed both Hubert Humphrey's hopes and his spirit had been crushed. Senate Democrats rejected him as their leader in favor of Sen. Robert Byrd of West Virginia. Even such supposed friends as AFL-CIO unionists had sided with Mr. Byrd. Sick and sick-at-heart, Sen. Humphrey was handed a consolation prize by the Senate: the odd title of deputy president pro tempore, a $7,400 raise and a chauffeured limousine.

At the time, it all seemed as demeaning as a cheap watch at retirement. But along with the honorary title and the fringe benefits came the right to attend all congressional leadership meetings, including those at the White House with President Carter. This gives Mr. Humphrey a way to exert his special kind of pressure.

The events of the past few months, in fact, seem to have put the 65-year-old liberal in a strong position to play the role of conscience prodder and idea-man. He is, in a new sense, free at last. He is free of the demands and the constraints of those seeking higher office, free to speak his conscience more clearly, free of needing always to think of the wishes of his none-too-loyal friends of the AFL-CIO, who abandoned him in the clutch. And finally, he is free of the suspicion and jealousy that attach to any politician who's believed to be reaching for the top.

"What I do from here on out," says Mr. Humphrey, "can't be self-serving, in terms of ambition." With a satisfied smile, he adds: "I'm going to be a lot more independent. I'm not planning on running for re-election. . . I'm not going to be making choices because I think, 'well, this will get me some votes from a particular category of people.' "

Humphrey-watchers in the Senate sense the difference already. "When he was going after the holy grail, he was always suspect," comments one veteran Democrat. "He no longer has that burden. When he speaks now, it is as a man who has no other place to go. And when he speaks, very few people leave the floor, and others begin drifting in."

That certainly has been true in recent days, as the master orator has captivated the galleries and his colleagues with eloquence and feeling. Senators actually stop talking to each other and listen (a rarity in the Senate) when Sen. Humphrey takes the floor.

The chamber grew hushed the other day when this man, who so barely missed being elected President in 1968, paid moving tribute to the man who so barely missed in 1976. He told of a private, post-election dinner in the White House, where Jerry and Betty Ford quietly shared with Hubert and Muriel Humphrey the exquisite pain that comes from going all-out, and losing.

You could sense, as Mr. Humphrey told of that evening, his unique ability to pour a balm of compassion on the wound of a political adversary. The old Democratic liberal recalled that he joked with the Republican President about their many clashes over economic and social policies, but then added: "History will not remember those things. . . . You will be remembered in history for having restored to the office of the presidency the decency, the honesty, the integrity, the honor, the nobility which that office must have."

Then, as the gaunt-looking figure dabbed at his eyes with a handkerchief, he added this: "And I said to him right then, 'I would have given five years of my life to have had two weeks, two months in this office, and you have had two-and-a-half years. You lost an election, but you haven't lost the love and respect of the American people.' " When Sen. Humphrey finished, the first man to jump up and pay tribute to him as "a decent man, a giant," was arch-conservative Republican Jesse Helms of North Carolina. There is no ideological chasm so wide that Mr. Humphrey can't bridge it.

The Senate listened intently last week too, as the Minnesotan engaged in a spirited, old-fashioned debate with Texas Republican John Tower over the power of of organized labor. Everyone on the floor knew what the AFL-CIO had done to its loyal supporter in his quest for the majority leadership: George Meany had passed the word that he supported Mr. Byrd, coldly siding with the expected winner rather than the old friend.

But you might have thought, hearing Sen. Humphrey speak, that he had a big debt to pay off to labor. He used his eloquence in generously chronicling the labor lobby's support of legislation for the poor, the hungry, the sick. He used humor in fending off Sen. Tower's thrusts at greedy unions: "Oh yes, I know, I hear about a plumber who makes $20,000 a year," declared Mr. Humphrey. "Well, who wants to go around cleaning out toilets and putting in pipes all the time? It is worth it." Thus old plumber George Meany is offered the other cheek, and Mr. Humphrey admits that's his way of shaming those who abandoned him.

The Senator relishes such debate. He loves to argue, and then to end the argument with a bear-hug, as he did with Sen. Tower. He loves the clash of ideas and the camaraderie of his fellows. And now he thinks he's in a position to capitalize on his ideas, his ability as a conciliator and the immense respect and affection flowing toward him in the Senate.

"I see my role," he says, "as a hard-working Senator, and an adviser, and a prodder." As a spokesman for the less-privileged of the country, he says, he plans "to push and shove a little, to prod and maybe to ask a little more than the times and conditions will permit. Unless you push and prod and ask, you're apt not to get even what you ought to get."

He knows he looks awful, but he insists he feels good, and it's obvious his spirit is unconquered. "Let's face it," he says, "if you have an operation for cancer, it is easy to give up. I've made up my mind not to give up. I heard a good minister say, 'It's not what you have lost, but what you've got left,' and I've got a lot left."

The only thing that irritates him is morose pity. "I told one reporter, 'just don't be in a hurry on the obituary. Don't print it too soon.' " Summoning the will to live isn't easy, he admits, "and then when somebody comes along and says. 'hey, you look like you're gonna die,' I just want to give him a big kick in the butt."

This is all said with good cheer and laughter, the unselfconscious bubbling of a still-young spirit. Sen. Humphrey loves living, and is convinced he still has much to contribute to the lives of others. All he needs is time. And it's a sure bet that anyone who knows the man would pray that he gets all the time he wants.

THE PERILS OF PRESIDENTIAL-CANDIDATE DEBATES

The Des Moines Sunday Register, February 12, 1984

If you are ever tempted to stage a presidential candidate debate, I have a word of advice: Don't. I have found myself deeply involved in presidential debates in three election years, and each time — when it was too late — I began asking myself: "What in the world am I doing here?"

The first experience, which should have been enough to permanently cure anyone's wish to participate in this media circus, came in 1976. Jimmy Carter was challenging incumbent president Jerry Ford that fall, and the League of Women Voters arranged a series of three debates between them. The League selected three journalists to question the candidates in the first debate — Elizabeth Drew, who writes for the New Yorker magazine; the late Frank Reynolds of ABC, and me. At the time, I was a Washington-based reporter for The Wall Street Journal.

Nothing about that Philadelphia debate is memorable except this: As it dragged toward its conclusion, the sound system went absolutely dead, leaving the candidates standing on stage, staring into the cameras in silence, for a full 28 minutes. It was network television's most colossal technical failure of

> ## Hello, hello, Mission Control? Any sign of Phil Donahue?

all time, first place in TV's hall of shame. But those 28 minutes may have been the most entertaining portion of the whole affair, and revealing, too: Ford and Carter never uttered a syllable to each other the whole time.

I asked a bunch of dull questions about taxes, budgets and the Federal

Reserve; only the answers were duller. Moments after the debate ended. Carter confessed to me that he had worried that the first question to him would be about "adultery" — because the debate occurred shortly after he told Playboy magazine that he had had "lust in his heart" for women. I left the stage thinking I'd missed a great opportunity.

The Register's 1980 Republican presidential candidate debate included, from left, Rep. Philip Crane of Illinois; Sen. Howard Baker of Tennessee; Rep. John Anderson of Illinois; former Gov. John Connally of Texas; Sen. Bob Dole of Kansas, and future president George H. W. Bush of Texas, with moderator James P. Gannon, center.

In 1980, a casual, breakfast table remark by my wife, Joan, ("Why don't you get all the candidates together in Iowa for a debate?") plunged me back into the game. An invitation to President Carter to come to Iowa to debate any Democratic challenger sat around the White House for 10 weeks without a response. The debate idea looked like a loser until the day before Ted Kennedy announced his candidacy; that day, the White House called to accept the invitation, challenging Kennedy to a debate before Kennedy could challenge Carter. In politics, timing is everything.

Once it seemed sure that there would be a Democratic debate in Iowa, all the Republican candidates jumped at the chance to share the network-TV spotlight in a separate GOP debate. All but one, that is. In a classic miscalculation, Ronald Reagan's campaign manager didn't like the idea of putting his candidate on stage with six others, so Reagan ducked The Register's debate —

a decision that probably cost him a victory in the Iowa caucuses, and one that cost his manager, John Sears, his job.

In the end, the Republicans came to debate, but the Democrats didn't. Jerry Brown muscled his way into the debate lineup by launching a quick storefront Iowa campaign, while Kennedy's poll ratings started falling, causing second-thoughts in the White House. After weeks of nit-picky negotiations with the participants (Kennedy wanted to stand during the debate, but Carter wanted to sit down — that sort of thing) the president called a week before the event to say he was really too busy with foreign policy to leave Washington. The 2,700 Democratic debate tickets that we'd mailed out became collector's items.

And now it is another election year, and unless something bizarre has happened, the headline of today's Sunday Register reports another debate showdown in Iowa. This column was written in those final countdown hours — the time of the sweaty palms — just before Saturday's Iowa Democratic debate.

You sit here wondering where Ted Koppel and Phil Donahue are when you really need them. But no, this is Iowa, not Hollywood. It just wouldn't do for Des Moines, of all places, to import show-biz; Iowa must present its plain, honest face, and if the nation yawns, it's not our problem.

The thing to do, it seemed to us, was to get the candidates on stage together and get the show-biz stars and the national journalists out of their way. Let them challenge each other in direct cross-examination, with no middlemen as filters. Let's find out who's aggressive and who's timid; who can think on the spot and who falls back on canned campaign phrases. Let's see if they'll sharply define their differences, or retreat into a comfortable, unified attack on Reagan.

That, anyway, was the idea. By now, you can judge whether it worked or not. As I write this, I feel some empathy for the astronaut perched atop a monster rocket as the clock ticks down to zero. Hello, hello, Mission Control? Any sign of Phil Donahue?

But it's too late again. Hold on tight, 1984 is here. And don't even think about 1988.

THE KEY TO POLITICS
IS COUNTRY MUSIC

The Des Moines Sunday Register, September 19, 1982

In my earlier days as a political reporter, I spent a good deal of time and effort searching out sources of political analysis and commentary. Washington was full of such sources: double-domed intellectuals, double-breasted diplomats, congressional staffers, pollsters, lobbyists, think-tankers and well-placed, usually reliable, deep background sources.

> I don't know if Reagan listens to country-music radio, though it would not surprise me if he does, because he understands the psychology of the country so well.

They all talked to journalists, and they all talked to each other, usually not for quotation, and the result was a marvelous circular process in which Washington talked to itself about itself with little relation to anyone else. Out of such a process would come penetrating columns of commentary about "the mood of the country."

The trouble with all of this was that none of the sources, and none of the journalists, ever listened to country-music radio stations.

It has taken me years to figure this out, but after being away from Washington for a while and gaining a new perspective on politics in America, the truth has finally been revealed: The best insight into the real America is gained against a background of twanging guitars on your local country-music station.

You may think this is a joke, but it is not. If you start listening carefully to the lyrics of country music — which Washington never does, because Washington does not care much for country music — you can get a handle on the political and economic situation better than George Gallup can with all his polls and computers.

This truth came to me the other night as Merle Haggard (note to Joseph Kraft: he is a country-music singer) mournfully captured in song the essential American political question of our time: "Are the good times really over for good?"

The song is something of a dirge, and it manages to encompass in its lamenting lyrics just about everything that's bothering everybody, from the decline in the economy to the collapse of the old morality. It recalls a happier day "when coke was a cola and a joint was a bad place to be," and when "a Ford or a Chevy would last 10 years, like they should."

You can't listen to this song without hearing just about every psychological reason why Ronald Reagan got elected in 1980. It makes you feel nostalgic for the 1950s and fearful for the 1980s, because it voices that gut-level worry that nags us all — that the good times may really be over for good.

I don't know if Reagan listens to country-music radio, though it would not surprise me if he does, because he understands the psychology of the country so well. If his basic 1980 campaign speech had been put to music in Nashville, it would have been a big country-radio hit. Reagan can wave the flag, ring the Liberty Bell and gush about small-town virtues better than any other politician alive. His heroes have always been cowboys.

Reagan had all the right lyrics in 1980 and mobilized the country-music vote into an electoral landslide. If you look at a map of the 1980 election returns, you'll find that Reagan's margins were biggest in places where country music is strongest. He was as popular as Waylon Jennings in the West, most of the South and non-urban areas in the North. Jimmy Carter, who got his campaign off to a good start by having Willie Nelson sing the national anthem at his nominating convention, lost touch with jukebox America and wound up carrying states like Rhode Island and Hawaii, where mommas don't let their babies grow up to be cowboys.

Now the 1982 midterm elections are fast approaching, and the key political question, which Washington hasn't even discovered yet, is whether Merle Haggard's song is working for or against Reagan. The uncloudy day that

Reagan promised in his 1980 campaign hasn't materialized. The economy remains sick, the world remains troubled and torn, and the rich get richer while the poor get poorer.

Reagan assured everybody in 1980 that the good times weren't really over for good — just over as long as big-spending Democrats ran the government — and most voters believed that, because they wanted to. Like Willie Nelson, Reagan's on the road again, with new lyrics to the same tune. The old song doesn't play as well the second time around.

Luckily for Reagan, however, the Democrats don't seem to understand the jukebox crowd at all, and they haven't come up with a good theme song for their own 1982 campaign. Reagan has handed them material that ought to be a smash hit, but they can't seem to get the music and the lyrics to mesh. If they can't get tuned in to a country-music frequency soon, it'll be blue eyes cryin' in the rain, come November.

And if you are baffled by all of this, you just aren't a country-music fan.

Jimmy Carter Looks Like the Herbert Hoover of 1980

The Des Moines Sunday Register, October 14, 1979

Herbert Hoover saw it coming. Two days after he took office as president in 1929, biographer David Burner reports, President Hoover "conferred with Federal Reserve officials about restraining stock speculation." In April, six months before the stock market crashed, Hoover asked newspaper editors to editorialize against stock speculation, and be took some steps to protect his own pocketbook.

In his recent biography titled, "Herbert Hoover, A Public Life," Burner discloses that Hoover "instructed his own financial agent, his friend Edgar Rickard, to liquidate certain of his personal holdings, 'as possible hard times are coming.' By May, when car sales had dipped and building slackened, he was switching to 'gilt-edged bonds.'"

Hoover asked banks to cut down on loans to speculators and asked the New York Stock Exchange to police itself more strictly. He also "came to fear that a sharp upward movement in the Federal Reserve discount rate might bring collapse," and he resisted the move for a time, before the Fed finally raised its leading rate, from 5 percent to 6 percent, in August 1929.

Hoover's moves on the eve of the Great Crash of 1929 make fascinating reading in this October exactly 50 years later, especially after a week in which the stock market reacted tumultously to the Federal Reserve's steps to

Fifty years after the Great Crash, Carter is in danger of being overwhelmed by economic events he can't control.

raise interest rates and restrict credit. This reading of history, against the back-drop of current storm-warnings in the economy, prompts the thought that Jimmy Carter may be the Herbert Hoover of our times.

The parallels in the lives of the two men are striking. Hoover was a strict Quaker moralist, a man risen up out of poverty in rural Iowa, who became an engineer, built up a reputation as a decent man, a humanitarian, and entered the presidency as a respected, well-liked figure. He was overwhelmed by economic events he could not control, and left the White House an embittered loser after one term.

Carter is a strict Baptist moralist, a man risen up out of poverty in rural Georgia, who became an engineer, built a reputation as a decent man, a humanitarian, and entered the presidency as a respected, well-liked figure. He now is in danger of being overwhelmed by economic events that be cannot control, which raises the prospect of his leaving the White House an embittered loser after one term.

Too much can be made of such parallels in character and events, of course.

President Jimmy Carter greets the author in the Cabinet Room of the White House, for an interview in November 1979.

This is 1979, not 1929, and this week's stock market turmoil was nothing so severe as the crash of that October a half-century ago. It would be foolish to predict another Great Depression, and it would be premature to say that Carter can't possibly survive what's likely to happen in economics and politics in the next 12 months.

Carter isn't Hoover, but then, neither is he Franklin D. Roosevelt. Note these lines from Burner's book:

"And this loner who relished a cooperative society distrusted Congress for being a collection of hungry, squabbling interests. He believed that as president he could transcend the mentalities of congressional factions and interests and make decisions like an engineer.... This aversion to congressional politics, this lack of feeling for the play of it, meant that he had to forego the uses to which the political strategist Franklin Roosevelt could put Congress in the articulating and orchestration of support for himself and his policies." Those lines were written about Hoover, but they apply equally well to Carter.

The president now faces an extremely difficult task in escaping Hoover's fate. The likely impact of the Federal Reserve's new tight-money policy makes Carter's chances for a political comeback even slimmer than they were just a week ago.

Over the next six to 12 months, the Fed's restrictive policy is expected to put the economy, and financial markets, through a wringer. The consensus among economists is that the mild recession that was already under way will be deepened and prolonged by the Fed's action. Interest rates are going topless, and the stock market may be going bottomless. Banks' prime lending rates, now at a record 14.5 percent, are likely to rise further, while home mortgage money becomes scarce and homebuilding heads down. Many economists are predicting sizable jumps in unemployment, to perhaps 8 percent or 9 percent in 1980, compared to less than 6 percent currently.

This may be needed medicine for an inflation fever, but the problem for Carter is that the payoff in terms of a lower inflation rate is likely to be slow in coming. The pain of the inflation cure will be sharp over the next few months — the politically critical period for the president — while the relief, if any, may come too late to help him much.

Carter has said he supports the Fed's tough anti-inflation policy, even though it seems to be playing right into the hand of Senator Edward Kennedy, who has said the economic issue will be crucial in his expected challenge of

Carter for the Democratic nomination. Kennedy, in almost-announcing his candidacy, has said the trends in unemployment, interest rates and recession would be the critical questions determining whether he would run. There has been almost no doubt of Kennedy's plan to run, and now Carter and the Fed have handed Kennedy this issue.

Carter faces the prospect of defending Republican-style economics on a Democratic playing field of primaries, which hardly seems fair. Unemployment, high interest rates and recession are dynamite issues in Democratic circles, and Kennedy will be playing offense with the wind at his back while Carter must play defense from a poor field position.

If he somehow survives the battle in his own party, Carter then will have to lead a deeply-divided party against the Republicans, who surely will charge economic mismanagement even though Carter has embraced an essentially Republican anti-inflation policy.

It's good politics to whip inflation rhetorically, but it remains to be seen whether it is good politics to try to actually whip inflation in an election year. Americans don't like inflation, but, in the past decade, they have learned to cope with it. If the price of arresting inflation is a combination of recession, unemployment and high interest rates, voters may decide that the cure is worse than the disease.

Carter told the nation in his press conference Tuesday that "whatever it takes to control inflation, that's what I will do." But two days later, he was telling leaders of AFL-CIO construction unions that "I will not fight inflation with your jobs" — the very jobs that are most likely to be lost to the tight-money policy that Carter says he supports.

Either the president is uncertain of his position or he is doing what he did during the 1976 campaign, which was to shade his position one way or another depending on his audience. Carter is kidding himself, or us, if he maintains that you can fight inflation with tight money and not hurt anybody.

Yes, Herbert Hoover saw it coming, but he couldn't do anything about it. You wonder if Carter even sees what's coming.

Just over a year after this column was written, Jimmy Carter lost the election of 1980 to Republican Ronald Reagan in a landslide, carrying only six states to Reagan's 44 states.

Will Reagan, like Truman, surprise us with greatness?

The Des Moines Sunday Register, January 4, 1981

Independence, Mo. – A visit to the Harry Truman presidential library here evokes memories of the past and questions about the future.

In a large room devoted to Truman's first six months as president, there's a collection of memorabilia that brings back dim boyhood memories: Franklin Roosevelt's funeral, the liberation of Berlin, the explosion of the first atomic bomb, V-J Day.

Truman's first few months in office truly were earth-shaking and earth-shaping. He became president on April 12, 1945, in a bleeding world of collapsing nations. Europe was a wreck, as Hitler's final defeat neared, and Asia remained a treacherous battlefield, as Japan refused to quit. A nightmare of war and a dream of peace were taking shape, as scientists put the finishing touches on the first nuclear weapon, and diplomats drafted plans for the United Nations.

Into this maelstrom was thrust a very ordinary man who proved to be extraordinary. He was a small-town Missouri boy, a farmer, a failure in business, a hack politician in the corrupt Kansas City Democratic Party machine. A party split let him squeak into the Senate, and another Democratic intramural squabble thrust him into the vice presidency as a compromise running mate for a dying FDR.

He never wanted to be more than a senator. On the day after he became president, he groaned to his friend, Senator George Aiken

> He [Truman] never wanted to be more than a senator.

127

of Vermont: "I am not big enough for this job." Nearly everybody agreed.

There is a quote from Truman mounted prominently on the wall of that room in his presidential library commemorating his first months as president. Truman, the day after he was sworn into the presidency, displayed his common touch and humility in this remark to reporters at the White House:

"Boys, if you ever pray, pray for me now. I don't know whether you fellas ever had a load of hay fall on you, but when they told me yesterday what had happened, I felt like the moon, the stars and all the planets had fallen on me. I've got the most terribly responsible job a man ever had."

You can't read that quote, in these days leading up to another inauguration, without wondering what Ronald Reagan is feeling, deep down inside, as he contemplates taking over "the most terribly responsible job a man ever had." Is he ready for it? Does he have the unrecognized reserves of courage, tenacity and common sense that made Truman a strong president? Is there much more to Ronald Reagan than we realize — a leadership quality that emerges, Truman-like, only after leadership is conferred?

We cannot know the answers to these questions before we live through them, unfortunately. There is a predisposition, in these days of national engagement prior to the Reagan honeymoon, to hope for the best. If a man who bungled the job of running a Kansas City haberdashery can become a great president, why not a genial fellow who made second-rate movies? (On the other hand, there was Warren G. Harding — but it is not nice to dwell on such thoughts in these pre-honeymoon days.)

It is possible to view the coming Reagan presidency through the prism of the Truman experience, though the men and the times are vastly different, and the prism may distort. Truman came to the presidency unprepared for it. He knew almost nothing about foreign affairs, his experience having been confined primarily to domestic political matters. He was no great intellect or scholar. He hadn't been to college. He liked poker, piano-playing, politics, bourbon, and sharing barracks tales with the boys. He was considered vulgar by the elite.

Robert J. Donovan, a veteran Washington newsman who covered Truman, wrote this summary of the man in "Conflict and Crisis," Donovan's excellent biography of HST: "In his beliefs, his ideals, his outlook, his reaction to things, Truman came close to being the typical self-made, white, middle-class

60-year-old American man of 1945." Change just two words and you have Reagan: "In his beliefs, his ideals, his outlook, his reaction to things, Reagan comes close to being the typical self-made, white, middle-class, 70-year-old American man of 1981."

Reagan won the presidency because he shares and can persuasively articulate the feelings of the common American on important issues: frustrated patriotism, suspicion of government, weariness with inflation and taxes, fear of moral and social decay, a yearning to be No. 1 again. If he can translate his perception of the popular will into policies that work, he will become a hero-president. He has that potential — but does he have that capacity?

Similar questions plagued Truman at the outset of his presidency. As quoted by Donovan, this is what Senator Arthur Vandenberg of Michigan wrote in his diary: "The gravest question-mark in every American heart is Truman. Can he swing the job? Despite his limited capacities, I think he can."

And so, at the start of 1981, the gravest question mark is Reagan. Can he swing the job? Don't look for the answer here. The best advice, in these days of doubt, is that which Harry Truman gave to the "boys" of the press: If you ever pray, pray for him — and for all of us — now.

Cruising toward Disaster: the Mondale Democrats of 1984

The Des Moines Sunday Register, June 10, 1984

Maybe what the Democratic Party really needs in 1984 is a good, sound whipping. And it's beginning to look as though the Democrats will get one, needed or not.

Those thoughts emerge as the party's leaders sort through the wreckage of the 1984 presidential primary season, trying to salvage enough working parts to piece together a political bandwagon while the rescue squad gives frantic first aid to the casualty who is supposed to drive the thing, Walter Mondale.

> **The Democrats again have managed to make an election-year mess of things.**

The other collision survivors, Gary Hart and Jesse Jackson, are off to the side licking wounds and snarling, still eyeing the broken steering wheel, while party bigwigs are shouting, "Get in the back seat, now!" It isn't a pretty sight, unless you are Ronald Reagan or another Republican politician up for election in November.

The Democrats again have managed to make an election-year mess of things, and just when the opposition seems to be getting all the breaks, from an improving economy to a spectacular exploitation of the advantages of incumbency, telecast in star-spangled color from the pubs of Ireland, the beaches of Normandy and the summit meetings in London.

It would have been hard for Walter Mondale to have beaten Ronald Reagan in 1984 even if he had breezed through the primaries, eliminated his competition early, and united the Democrats for a love-in at the national convention next month. But now, after a bitterly divisive fight through all the caucuses and primaries, in which Mondale's weaknesses have been ruthlessly exposed by his challengers, the task looks nearly impossible. Mondale, now almost certain to be the Democratic nominee even though he lost more primaries than he won, must suddenly become Harry Truman to win. He's never been confused with the man from Missouri, and isn't likely to be now.

You would think that the party leaders and convention delegates, who are savvy enough to know these political realities, now would search for some alternative to nominating a heavily damaged likely loser. You would think that if you were a logical, common-sense person — but probably not if you really were a delegate or party boss.

Those people know that the Democratic Party is a myth. It isn't one party but a loose coalition of mini-parties, each with a separate agenda and each clinging tenaciously to its lever of control. The forces that dominate the primaries, and will control the convention, are the powerful mini-parties: organized labor, incumbent officeholders, blacks, unionized teachers, feminists, Jews, senior citizens.

The mini-parties think less about winning elections than they do about maintaining their influence over party processes, platform and the nominee. Certainly, Lane Kirkland, leader of the AFL-CIO, wants to oust Reagan from the White House, but he would be aghast at the thought of trying it with Gary Hart, with whom he has scant influence. A President Hart could thumb his nose at Kirkland's special-interest agenda.

The blacks would love to see Jesse Jackson on the national ticket, but the Jews, who find him insufficiently committed to Israel, wouldn't stand for it. You can go down the list and find these narrow interests dominant with each group; you cannot find important forces within the party thinking primarily about ways to win the votes of the great masses of Democrats not committed to any mini-party, or especially, of independent or Republican voters. Bluntly put, minorities do not think of the majority.

Mondale will win the nomination because he has collected more of the mini-parties behind him than anyone else. He will build the platform they want, select a running mate they can all accept, and he will campaign on their collective agendas.

Except for stirring fears of what Ronald Reagan might do in a second term, he will not have much to say to generic Democrats, or independents, or non-Reaganite Republicans — most of whom find themselves outside the orbit of the mini-parties.

It would take a crashing defeat of Mondale to expose the Democratic party as a myth and to undermine the influence of the mini-parties. A debacle on the order of the Barry Goldwater loss that the GOP suffered in 1964 would shock Democrats into the realization that the dominance of special interests has pulled their party out of line with the broader interests of the majority of Americans.

A Mondale disaster would close an era that began with the New Deal in the 1930s and began looking obsolete in the 1970s, and would open the party to a new generation of ideas and leaders.

The election of 1984, Mondale vs. Reagan, thus represents the last, desperate gamble of the old order. Right now, it looks like a losing bet for the Democrats. Such a loss would be painful for the party, but it may be the only way the Democrats will be able to free themselves from the bondage of the past and the special interests, and begin forging a majoritarian agenda for the future.

Five months after this was written, Mondale and the Democrats suffered the expected disaster, losing 49 states (all except Mondale's Minnesota) in the Reagan re-election landslide of November 1984.

6

WAR & PEACE

"Running in the rain, back to the National Press Building, you think of young men the age of your sons, in the skies over Iraq and Kuwait, risking death. Your sons are safe, but some fathers and mothers now share the agony of waiting, wondering if theirs will come back alive.

Now it's real. Something rises in your throat to tell you. This is how it feels when a war starts. You can know it's coming, and still it stuns."

LENINGRAD: A SURVIVOR THAT NEVER FORGETS

The Des Moines Sunday Register, August 3, 1986

Leningrad, USSR - As you enter this city that suffered so brutally during a 900-day Nazi siege during World War II, you come upon a moving memorial to the courage and suffering of the Russian people in what they call "the Great Patriotic War."

The memorial rises in the center of a major boulevard into the city from the airport, situated to arrest the eye of every visitor. It is a work of terrible beauty, in which the stark, gray sculptures of Leningrad's heroes — soldiers, factory women, starving mothers and children — seem yet to weep.

The Russian people know war in a way that we Americans do not.

Leningrad does not let anyone — especially foreign visitors — forget what it went through in the last world war. For 900 days and 900 nights, it was besieged and bombarded by the Germans. More than one million of its residents died from the shelling, the sickness, the starvation and the bitter winter cold of those terrible years, 1941-44. But Leningrad never surrendered. It endured. It triumphed. It does not forget.

In a bunker-like museum below the ground-level memorial, the mementos of war are displayed — rusty weapons, diaries of soldiers and children, a tiny loaf of hard, black "bombardment bread" that was the only food that millions had during the siege. The museum is lit by 900 flickering electric torches — each made from a spent artillery shell.

World War II lives on in Russia. The war that is mostly a fading memory in

America is a living part of the present-day consciousness of people in the Soviet Union — in a way that is startling to Americans. The memory of the war and its meaning seems woven into the fabric of Soviet life.

There are many reminders — not only in numerous memorials but in people. On the streets of Moscow and Leningrad, it is commonplace to see the men of World War II - now mostly gray-haired or bald — who proudly wear their veterans' ribbons and medals on the breasts of their suit-coats. The defenders of Russia proudly proclaim themselves publicly, in a way that would be considered slightly bizarre in America. Here, it is a badge of honor to wear the decorations of war.

This war-consciousness is more than nostalgia. It is a pervasive influence on the psychology of this country. Russians constantly remind visitors that 20 million Soviet citizens died in World War II. Nearly every family was touched directly by that loss. They remember. And they want us to remember.

In my conversations with Russians, there were constant references to that war, and to the determination of the Soviet people never to let it happen again. You can write some of this off as propaganda intended to impress an American newspaperman, I suppose, but I cannot dismiss it all as just that. The Russian people know war in a way that we Americans do not. Their dread of the idea seems genuine. If we had lost 20 million of our fellow citizens would we not feel the same?

They speak constantly of their thirst for peace. It gets more than a bit annoying, this drumbeat of peace talk, as if the Russians were the only people with an interest in peace.

An yet they seem to genuinely fear America, and to believe that our government and our military-industrial complex is determined to accelerate an arms race that is all too likely to end in nuclear war. They are especially afraid of our program for space-based "Star Wars" weapons. They do not believe that President Reagan's program is defensive. They are sure that any space weapons will become an offensive threat to them.

I am convinced that their fear is real, and that they are determined to do whatever it takes to keep abreast or ahead of the United States militarily. I don't believe they can be out-spent and overtaken. They will make great sacrifices domestically to maintain military parity or superiority. As one U.S. diplomat put it: "You can't expect to spend them into submission. This is a country that can live very low on the hog."

Very low, indeed. They lived on tiny black loaves of bread to survive the last world war. To prevent another one, they will do whatever necessary to match our military capabilities. Perhaps a keener memory of wars past would serve us well, too.

OUR WARS ARE NEVER CLEAR-CUT ANYMORE

The Des Moines Sunday Register, October 2, 1983

The U.S. Marines are back in the headlines, on the nightly television newscasts, on the news-magazine covers. Another battlefield, another war, stretching over time's horizon from Guadalcanal, Tarawa, Iwo Jima and Okinawa through Vietnam and now to Beirut.

From one war to another, the Marines at the front always look alike — young, strong men in camouflage uniforms, with the tense readiness of a tightly wound steel coil — whether the picture is of Guam in 1944 or Da Nang in 1966 or Beirut in 1983. But the looks may be deceiving.

World War II was the last clear-cut, all-out crusade for a certain objective . . . by a generation of men and women who knew — by God, they absolutely knew — exactly what they were doing and exactly why it had to be done, at all costs.

Beirut is no Vietnam, and certainly not the vast Pacific theater of World War II, and the reasons for our Marines being there — in the midst of an endless civil war — seem much less clear than in those previous engagements. There may be some vital U.S. interest in trying to make a nation out of a three- or four-sided death struggle called Lebanon, but if so, it has not been adequately articulated by our leaders. There may also be some role for the Marines beyond being a sandbagged target serving as the trip-wire for wider involvement, but if so, it seems unclear.

You can't help wondering what these Marines are thinking, and writing home to their families, or saying to each other behind the sandbag walls. They are in a puzzling situation that has become the subject of a political minuet in Washington, with the president and the Congress dancing around the perimeters of a congressional resolution that neither declares war nor rejects it, leaving unanswered all the large questions about why and what and how long.

Our wars are never clear-cut any more. Vietnam, Central America, Lebanon — all seem a rather gauzy, muddled effort to project U.S. power in places where it may or may not help, in ways that seem designed to struggle against poor odds. World War II was the last clear-cut, all-out crusade for a certain objective, fought in a way that wars will never be fought again, by a generation of men and women who knew — by God, they absolutely knew — exactly what they were doing and exactly why it had to be done, at all costs.

Nothing that I have seen or read has better demonstrated this vast difference between the old wars and the new ones, and between the generations that fought them, than a book by William Manchester that has been my evening companion lately. In "Goodbye Darkness — A Memoir of the Pacific War," Manchester weaves an intensely personal tapestry of the struggle in the Pacific theater, of the men whom he fought with there as a young Marine, and of the vast chasm that now separates that time, that world and the values and goals that prevailed then from the uncertainties that mark the present and haunt the future.

It would be a travesty to pretend to summarize Manchester's memoir, which takes its emotional power from the careful piling on of the incredible facts of the Pacific war, the feelings of fear, pride, hate, pain, sorrow and numbness that were the lot of the fighting men. A reader who had only a young boy's-eye view of World War II, but has watched the subsequent development of our modern, uncertain wars, comes away awed that there was a generation of American men capable of coping with its horrors, and willing and able to see it through to its end.

Near the end of his memoir, which was finished in 1980 after the author had completed an island-by-island re-visitation of the Pacific battlefields of the Marines, Manchester tries to sort out his feelings, and explain how it was that young Americans faced and endured that trial.

In doing so, he describes the generation that fought in 1942-45, and how their backgrounds made it possible:

"To fight in World War II you had to have been tempered and strengthened in the 1930s Depression by a struggle for survival — in 1940, two out of every five draftees had been rejected, most of them victims of malnutrition. And you had to know that your whole generation, unlike the Vietnam generation, was in this together, that no strings were being pulled for anybody; the four Roosevelt brothers were in uniform, and the sons of both Harry Hopkins, FDR's closest adviser, and Leverett Saltonstall, one of the most powerful Republicans in the Senate, served in the Marine Corps as enlisted men and were killed in action.

". . .(you) had to remember your father's stories about the Argonne, and saying your prayers, and Memorial Day, and Scouting, and what Barbara Fritchie said to Stonewall Jackson. And you had to have heard Lionel Banrymore as Scrooge and to have seen Gary Cooper as Sergeant York. And seen how your mother bought day-old bread and cut sheets lengthwise and re-sewed them to equalize wear while your father sold the family car, both forfeiting what would be considered essentials today so that you could enter college.

"You also needed nationalism, the absolute conviction that the United States was the envy of all the other nations, a country which had never done anything infamous, in which nothing was insuperable, whose ingenuity could solve anything by inventing something. . . Wickedness was attributed to flaws in individual character, not to society's shortcomings. To accept unemployment compensation, had it existed, would have been considered humiliating. . . Debt was ignoble. Courage was a virtue. Mothers were beloved, fathers obeyed.

"Marriage was a sacrament. Divorce was disgraceful. Pregnancy meant expulsion from school or dismissal from a job. . . Couples did not keep house before they were married, and there could be no wedding until the girl's father approved. . . . You needed a precise relationship between the sexes, so that no one questioned the duty of boys to cross the seas and fight while the girls wrote them cheerful letters. from home . . .

"All this led you into battle, and sustained you as you fought, and comforted you if you fell, and, if it came to that, justified your death to all who loved you as you had loved them. Later the rules would change. But we didn't know that then. We didn't know."

It's not only the wars that are different. We are different. The world is different. Iwo Jima, and the men who fought there, are on the other side of an invisible divide. Do you suppose that the Marines in Beirut, huddled behind their sandbags, have any concept of this?

Seeing "Platoon" With Your Teenage Son Stirs Guilt and Fear

The Des Moines Sunday Register, February 8, 1987

> **"Platoon" is a movie that reaches a peak of tension in the opening minutes and simply does not relent until the final frame.**

Last weekend, I took my 15-year-old son Chris to see "Platoon," the movie about life and death as a combat soldier in Vietnam. I wasn't at all sure I wanted to see it, and not sure if I should take my teenager to it. The reviews had convinced me that it would be more anguish than entertainment. That it was. "Platoon" is a movie that reaches a peak of tension in the opening minutes and simply does not relent until the final frame. There is no relief, just as there must have been no relief, day or night, in the 24-hour-a-day war of the Asian jungle.

I've never seen a film affect an audience the way this one does. When it ended, many were weeping. Quite a few just sat in their seats after it was over, immobilized, silent, struggling to regain composure. As the audience slowly and silently spilled into the lobby of the theater, the crowd behind the velvet ropes, waiting to get into the next showing, stared at us. You could see them looking us over, as if we were alien creatures. They saw the pain and sorrow on the faces emerging from the dark theater, and suddenly their bubbly conversations stopped, and they watched us, as if to ask: "My God, what happened in there?"

The answer to that question is an individual, private thing. So much of what you get from "Platoon" depends on what you bring to it.

I had brought a dulled memory of that terrible war, and long-suppressed feelings of shame and guilt. It has been, what — 20 years? So much of the ache of that time had ebbed away, a distant pain over some dark horizon behind us. "Platoon" packages that ache in a two-hour punch to the soft underbelly of the conscience.

I had not gone to Vietnam. I was married and a father and draft-deferred, and a bit too old. My friends did not go, either. People like us generally did not go. We were white and well-off and college graduates with good jobs. We stayed home.

That is part of the pain of "Platoon." It reminds us who fought that hopeless war. The "grunts" of the combat platoons were disproportionately black, or underclass white — high-school graduates or dropouts. The Selective Service System seemed to select those that society deemed had the least to lose, and we shipped them to the jungle — where many of them lost it all, and the rest lost pieces of their bodies and souls.

That was a mockery of democracy, one that made Vietnam a double shame for America. The worldwide shame was what we did to that country, after it became clear that there was no winning — only destruction — to be done there. The national shame was that we sent our "expendable" people to do it for us. If this sounds like guilt, it is. It is the nation's guilt, and "Platoon" brings it to painful life.

There was something particularly anguishing about watching this movie while sitting next to a son emerging from boyhood into manhood. Those soldiers on the screen were only three or four years older than he is now.

I could not help fearing a real-life rerun of the Vietnam experience. Are the jungles of Central America the next killing ground for our sons? Lyndon Johnson said he'd never send American boys to do the job Asian boys must do; Ronald Reagan promises that aiding the Nicaraguan rebels will never lead to use of U.S. troops in Central America. In the dark of the theater, a father remembers and worries.

Still, I felt it was good for Chris to see this film. He later told me it was the best movie he's ever seen, one that took the glory and fun out of war. He and his generation have grown up on "Rambo" and Clint Eastwood films, which make killing a video game. In "Platoon," my son saw war and death in a different, melancholy light — not as entertainment but as a much-too-real wasting of young men much like himself. I doubt that the next "Rambo" movie will have quite the same appeal to him now.

This is not a recommendation that you see "Platoon" nor that you bring a child with you. It is not entertainment. Perhaps only Catholics will understand this, but seeing "Platoon" is reminiscent of the feeling I remember many years ago in going to confession. It dredges up our sins, and forces the terrible question: Good God, how could we have done this?

"Platoon" combines the dread and relief of a long-delayed confession. It asks us to forgive each other, and to go and sin no more.

BOB CHASTEK SURVIVED VIETNAM, BUT IN THE END, IT KILLED HIM

The Detroit News, February 11, 1990

In the last few summers of his life, Bob Chastek sought peace in the north woods of Minnesota.

"He went up north during summers to help take care of resorts, mowing lawns," his mother Margaret recalled in St. Louis Park, Minn. "He had to be outdoors. Nature was quieter for him. Here at my house it was noisy — cars backfiring, and planes going over. ... It was better for him outside." The peace Bob Chastek hungered for was an elusive thing in the 19 years after he returned from war. Vietnam was the pivot point of his life, upon which everything swiveled. The half-life lived after the war was the dark side of his 39 years.

You could picture Bob Chastek playing himself in one of those war movies where the platoon always includes a certain cast of characters. He was the Minnesota farm boy — tall, gangly, earnest, hardworking, obedient to duty.

When he felt the draft bearing down in 1969, he enlisted in the Army and volunteered for helicopter training. Bob was "always interested in flying," his mother said. "He could fix anything that had a motor running."

It took some winking at the rules to

> Last week, his mother received a card from President Bush, expressing his sympathy, and saluting Bob Chastek, a Minnesota farm boy, for his service to the country.

get the lanky 19-year-old into a helicopter outfit. "He was too tall, but they needed them so desperately that they showed him how to stoop so he would fit," his mother said. "He grew more after he got in, but when he finished he was six-six. Long arms and long body."

They made him a door gunner on the big Huey choppers that ferried U.S. troops in and out of battle zones. It was a horrible job. Margaret describes the routine: "They took them out and left them off. And then they would go back to get them, and they would be in pieces."

Bob Chastek put in his year-long tour of duty, surviving against the odds in a high-risk job. Then he signed up for another six months. He was wounded and hospitalized, but wanted to finish his tour. "He could have come home, I guess, but he didn't want to leave his group there," his mother explained.

What Bob Chastek saw in Vietnam haunted the rest of his life.

It was in those final months he saw his closest friends die. "That's when his buddies got it, in the last six months, but he didn't," Margaret said. "And I said, several times in the last three years, he should have died in Vietnam with them, because he couldn't ever get over them."

When he returned home, his war should have been over — but in its most devastating effect, it was just beginning. Margaret remembered: "When he got off in San Diego, they spit at him — the protesters. He couldn't figure out what in the hell was going on back here, he said. He couldn't get it. Never did. He said, 'God, I didn't go over there because I wanted to. I was sent.' It was rough for him. He had so much pain."

Then the nightmares began.

"The nightmares just drove him. He was afraid to sleep. It got worse and worse instead of better," Margaret said. He tried counseling offered by the Veterans Administration. "They meant well but it just didn't fill it. His hurt was too deep. His pain was too deep."

His life became a series of odd jobs and unfinished things, interrupted by nightmares.

"I remember one time when I opened the door when I heard him thrashing around and yelling and groaning," Margaret said. "My curtains were wound around his long arm. I startled him. And if he'd have had a hand grenade or a gun in his hand, he would have shot me, not knowing who I was. I never opened the door again.   But I would wake him by rapping and pounding on the door."

At night, his mind replayed the videotape of Vietnam, over and over. He was back in the combat zone, pulling wounded GIs into the chopper.

Scenes from the videotape now live with Margaret.

"This one particular buddy had both arms and legs shot off, and Bob held him in his arms . . . and he kept yelling at Bob, 'Push me out the door! I can't go home like this. Push me out! Push me out!' Bob heard him until the last."

The end came two weeks ago in the bedroom of his mother's home, when the door gunner ended his nightmares with one final pull on the trigger of a gun.

They won't make a movie about Bob Chastek. He wasn't born on the fourth of July, and he didn't become a war protester. He did his duty in war and never found tranquility in peace. Last week, his mother received a card from President Bush, expressing his sympathy, and saluting Bob Chastek, a Minnesota farm boy, for his service to the country.

WAR'S FIRST IMAGES:
THE SOUND OF RAIN, THE SOUND OF PROTEST, THE SOUND OF BOMBS

The Detroit News, January 20, 1991

Running in the rain. That's how it began, running in the rain to the White House. You remember this from another time, long ago. Why is it always dark and rainy at these moments? The sidewalk in front of the Treasury is slick. Don't fall and break a leg. There's a long night ahead.

> **Bush watches the war on TV; probably Saddam Hussein does, too.**

Police have roped off the sidewalk in front of the president's house. A cop in a slicker is grabbing an old woman trying to push aside a saw-horse barricade. "Lady, if you do that again, I'm gonna have to arrest you."

Across Pennsylvania Avenue into Lafayette Park. A cluster of young protesters chant: "One, two, three, four, we don't want your (bleeping) war." For a moment, life seems trapped in a mad VCR running on fast-backwards: The film is deja vu, starring Nixon, Vietnam and protesters in this park, and you are running in the rain in 1971.

No, wake up. That's George Bush across the street, it's 1991, and these kids in the park are smiling, having fun. Their first chance to protest. They don't even remember Vietnam.

Trot across Pennsylvania, through the northwest gate, into the press briefing room. Mob scene: Reporters in wet raincoats scramble for seats, photographers block aisles with aluminum stepladders they climb to shoot over the mob. Everyone knows what's coming. TV reporters in Baghdad already are reporting anti-aircraft fire and bombing. It is 6:58 p.m., Wednesday, Jan.16, 1991.

You knew in your heart it was coming seven hours ago, when Marlin Fitzwater, Bush's spokesman, read a poignant personal letter to the press, imploring news organizations to get their reporters out of Baghdad "at once." He knew the bombs were soon to fall.

Fitzwater enters, looking like his dog just died. He reads a statement he wrote a day earlier: "The liberation of Kuwait has begun." Churchillian in tone, it takes just 35 seconds, and it changes the world.

Running in the rain, back to the National Press Building, you think of young men the age of your sons, in the skies over Iraq and Kuwait, risking death. Your sons are safe, but some fathers and mothers now share the agony of waiting, wondering if theirs will come back alive.

Now it's real. Something rises in your throat to tell you. This is how it feels when a war starts. You can know it's coming, and still it stuns.

This is the best advertised war in history, timed to a deadline, scripted even in the way it would begin with air assaults. So predictable, yet totally unpredictable.

It's TV's war now. For the first hours, it had the old-timey feel of a radio war, as if this were London under the blitz, with CNN's crew in Baghdad doing Edward R. Murrow-style audio descriptions of bombardment.

But quickly, 1940 fades and 1991 is on our screens: a live, as-it-happens, audience-participation war that knits the global village together. Bush watches the war on TV; probably Saddam Hussein does, too.

The new images of war: cruise missiles roaring brightly into the night. Electronic "smart bombs" falling precisely on target, watched by a TV camera on the plane. TV correspondents frantically donning gas masks, narrating a missile attack on Israel in muffled voices,

This is real. When you turn off your TV set, it goes on. This is life now: We can't change channels, even if the program in days ahead turns grim. Our bubble of euphoria over the first day's success burst quickly when a whole nation, Israel, had to don gas masks.

The script for the first chapter of this war was written in the Pentagon but the rest of the story may have to be written in the desert, day by day, by nearly a million authors who wear foot soldiers' gear.

This will not be another Vietnam. Bush has promised. And it looks nothing like Vietnam in its opening stages. What we don't know, however, is whether it will be another Verdun. Or Guadalcanal. Or Korea. If it comes, a grinding ground war in the desert holds unknown losses.

The liberation of Kuwait has begun. What price we will pay to finish it is unclear. The president's Friday warning against over-optimism is sobering advice that hints of sacrifice in days to come.

At times in a long journalistic career, the sense of déjà vu is overwhelming. So it was the night the Persian Gulf war began in 1991, when the situation threw me back to my days of running to the White House to cover news of the Vietnam War twenty years earlier.

WHERE IS THE SENSE OF DUTY THAT UNITED AMERICA IN WORLD WAR II?

Gannett News Service, April 30, 1995

Among the souvenirs of my youth is a yellowed copy of the Minneapolis Times of Monday, May 7, 1945. Headlines six inches tall proclaim: "Nazis Quit—War in Europe Over."

I was six years old at the time, so my memories of World War II are limited. I remember the "blackouts" when sirens wailed, and an air-raid warden wearing a helmet came down our street in Minneapolis to make sure all our lights were off, so enemy bombers could not see their target. It seems silly now, but it was part of the total mobilization of America toward one goal — winning the biggest war in world history.

I remember ration stamps that permitted our family only limited quantities of sugar, coffee, gasoline and other scarce commodities, and "Victory Gardens" for home-grown food. I remember collecting tin cans and other scrap metal for the war effort. And I remember being sure of one thing, that America would win the war.

It was the last time Americans were totally united and mobilized toward a common purpose.

As the 50th anniversary of victory in Europe approaches, these childhood memories hold a meaning and a message that is far more profound than I understood at the time. The defeat of Nazi Germany — and, three months later, imperial Japan — was the result of a united, total effort by every American citizen, from school children to retirees, in every community across the country. It was the last time Americans were totally united and mobilized toward a common purpose.

Writing of D-Day, the June 6, 1944 invasion of Normandy that led to Germany's defeat, historian Stephen E. Ambrose, recalls that unity. "On D-Day, a vast majority of the American people was involved. Most of them had made a direct contribution, as farmers providing the food, as workers in defense plants making planes or tanks or shells or rifles or boots.... or as volunteers doing the work at hundreds of agencies. The bandages they had rolled, the rifles they had made, were being put to use even as they heard the news. They prayed that they had done it right."

It was a time of unselfish sacrifice, uncommon courage, unprecedented persistence, and unashamed patriotism. The enemy was so clear, and so clearly evil, and the Allied cause was so just, and so imperative, that there was no room for doubt or division. American men and women did whatever was needed to win the war, with trust in their fellow citizens and their government that seems unimaginable today.

Dwight Eisenhower, the hero-general of the war in Europe, captured the spirit of that time in a televised conversation with Walter Cronkite 20 years after D-Day. Looking out over Omaha Beach, Ike remarked that "it is a wonderful thing to remember what those fellows 20 years ago were fighting and sacrificing for, what they did to preserve our way of life. Not to conquer any territory, not for any ambitions of our own. But to make sure that Hitler could not destroy freedom in the world."

How much we Americans have changed in this half-century. The society that defeated fascism in the 1940s was not perfect, to be sure. Racial segregation and discrimination were widespread and officially enforced, millions of Americans lived in poverty, and women who filled the assembly lines of war factories soon found that they were expected to get back in the kitchen when the men came home needing jobs.

The post-war era produced progress in all those areas, but something precious was lost along the road of peace, prosperity and diversity that we have traveled these last 50 years. Could America ever unite and mobilize now as it did then? Would Americans sacrifice their comforts, riches, careers and even their lives to fight for freedom—especially to fight an enemy not at our shores but threatening our allies abroad? Would 1990s Americans answer the call of their government the way 1940s Americans did?

I would like to think so, but I doubt it. I am not sure we would come out of the bunkers we have built for ourselves as feminists and angry white men, as liberals and conservatives, as blacks who see racism in everything white and whites who fear everyone black, as organized, suspicious, self-centered senior citizens or Generation X-ers or environmentalists or gun lovers.

We have become a nation of factions and causes, united only in our suspicion and mistrust of one another. Occasionally a galvanizing event, such as the bombing in Oklahoma City, produces a kind of television-synthesized sense of caring and community, but as surely as TVs attention will wane, the sense of togetherness will fade. Next week's story may be about whether white rescue workers got more camera time than black rescue workers.

More than anything else, America needs to recapture its sense of oneness and its feeling of community and common purpose. Fifty years after V-E Day, this is the greatest challenge the nation faces. Lacking the unifying effect of an external enemy, Americans must create a sense of community and common purpose in identifying and fighting an enemy within.

The lack of respect for life that animated Hitler's conquest of Europe is reborn today it the streets of America, where murder runs rampant and citizens cower in their homes, as they did when Nazis marched. The bombing of innocent citizens, even children, by home-grown terrorists is as hateful as the Luftwaffe's bombing of Allied cities.

If today's Americans have inherited any of the World War II generation's sense of duty and unity, this epidemic of American-made violence is an enemy worthy of a total mobilization effort. It will take the spirit that won the war 50 years ago to restore the peace in the nation today.

7

THE NEWSPAPER LIFE

"After 21 years in this business, I have begun to understand that a newspaper is a most complex and curious institution. It is a business. It is a work of art. It is a political force, a cultural expression, a sociological mirror, a cornerstone of democracy, a slice of history, a cheap education, a good companion."

A NEW EDITOR'S THOUGHTS ON NEWSPAPERS AND LIFE IN JOURNALISM

The Des Moines Sunday Register, September 5, 1982

Twenty-one years ago tomorrow — on September 6, 1961 — a young fellow just out of journalism school walked into a newspaper office in Chicago and sat down behind an old manual typewriter. He was given some copy paper, some fat yellow pencils and an inconsequential assignment. He was scared stiff.

The boss, a lean-and-hungry-looking Scotsman who appeared to have walked out of a Charles Dickens tale, told him he had six months to prove himself as a reporter. Like a rookie trying to break into the National Football League, the kid was trying to make the starting lineup of The Wall Street Journal, and he had to get through a six-month probation period to make it. His every move would be watched by the Scotsman with the eagle eyes.

The kid knew nothing about economics or business, and suddenly he was tossed into a strange new world of balance sheets, dividends, banking, commodity futures and corporate jargon. "Sink or swim" was what the boss said.

His heart sank and he treaded water for six months. He made two dreadful mistakes that required corrections in the newspaper, and an irate top editor in New York told the kid's boss that one more would put the kid down for the

> **A newspaper is a political force, a cultural expression, a sociological mirror, a cornerstone of democracy, a slice of history, a cheap education, a good companion.**

third time. His stories were all rewritten by the boss.

His big assignment — the one designed to see if the kid could spot a trend that might make a Page One feature — was to cover a convention of plumbing manufacturers in search of a snappy new look at the latest developments in water closets and shower heads. He couldn't find a story in it, though he still remembers the names of all the key makers of commodes and brass fittings. He finally made Page One, just as the probationary period ended, with a story out of Le Sueur, Minnesota, on the Green Giant Company's snappy new trends in pea-picking and pea-packing.

I was that kid. That was a long time ago, but the memory is as vivid as yesterday. I survived the probationary period — just barely — and suffered through a couple more years of apprenticeship under the dour Scotsman, John McWethy. I later came to understand that he was a great teacher of reporters and a man with a well-hidden soft heart. He taught me — and a generation of Wall Street Journal reporters — more about the gathering and writing of news than anyone else I ever encountered.

At age 22, I began pounding out stories on an old manual typewriter in my first full-time job as a reporter in the Chicago Bureau of The Wall Street Journal.

After a couple of years of stories about plumbing supplies and pea-picking, the assignments got better. Chicago, brawny city of the big shoulders, served up well-muscled business stories of railroad strikes, packinghouse closings, black unemployment. Pittsburgh, murky milltown on the Monongahela River, provided boom-and-bust tales of economic recession, urban renewal, coal-mine disasters and steel-industry union fights. None of it was light reading, but it was a good education in the America that was evolving, in the 1960s and early 1970s.

And then there was

Washington and Nixon and Watergate. From 1972 on, I had a chance to report and interpret the amazing roller-coaster ride that was American politics and government and economics in the 1970s. In my mind's eye, I still can see Nixon standing stiffly in the Oval Office, trying hard to be cordial to a bunch of White House reporters he hated; George Shultz at the Treasury, announcing a dollar devaluation or a freeze on wages and prices; Jimmy Carter frying catfish at a picnic in Plains, Ga., before a battery of network television cameras; Hubert Humphrey on the Senate floor, emaciated with cancer, saying a final farewell to his colleagues, who wept at the sight.

That was all before I came to Iowa. In the past four years, with the help and support of my friend and mentor, Michael Gartner, I have learned much about Iowa and The Des Moines Register, about what this state is and what this newspaper should be.

I have learned from Gartner, and from more than 200 proud, professional people on our news staff, what it takes to produce a good newspaper. And I have learned from others how much it is the product of hundreds of minds and hearts and hands — those of printers and pressmen, ad sellers and newsprint buyers, truck dispatchers and young boys and girls on bicycles.

After 21 years in this business, I have begun to understand that a newspaper is a most complex and curious institution. It is a business. It is a work of art. It is a political force, a cultural expression, a sociological mirror, a cornerstone of democracy, a slice of history, a cheap education, a good companion.

To those of us in this business, a newspaper is a precious thing. It is not something to be tampered with lightly. It is not just another consumer product, like toothpaste or detergent, to be renamed and repackaged, fortified with synthetic ingredients and test-marketed in supermarkets. A newspaper, instead, is an integral part of our culture and civilization — an irreplaceable thread woven into the fabric of our economy, politics and society.

Those are heavy thoughts — a long way from agonizing over stories on pea-picking — but they come to mind now as a new era begins to unfold here. As a story on the front page of today's Sunday Register reports, this newspaper is naming a new publisher, Gary Gerlach, and a new editor, yours truly. On Sept. 27, we will introduce a new, revamped newspaper under an old, revered name — The Des Moines Register. The new paper will combine the best of the present Register and its sister paper, the Des Moines Tribune, which will cease to exist as a separate entity.

In coming days and weeks, we will have much more to say about what this change will mean to our readers and advertisers. For now, it is enough to state a simple, but ambitious, personal goal: to put out the best daily newspaper ever published in Iowa, one worthy of a grand tradition and national recognition.

There are a few points in a lifetime when you look back at all that has happened and look forward to all that is possible, and this is one of those times for me. If you have read this far, I thank you for indulging my nostalgia, and I hope you share my faith that tomorrow's promise is always brighter than yesterday's record.

A BRIGHT, SHINING MOMENT IN THE NUT-HOUSE OF NEWSPAPER JOURNALISM

The Des Moines Sunday Register, April 28, 1985

Working in a newsroom is an odd occupation. It attracts a peculiar sort of person who enjoys hanging around a roomful of desks that look like trash dumps, where an average dinner is a brown-bag sandwich eaten in occasional bites while you cradle a phone against your ear and hammer the keys of a computer terminal, usually swearing or smoking in between bites.

You do this while your spouse and kids wonder why you never come home from the office until either you or they are too tired to care. You do this for as many years as your stomach and your mind can stand it, and then you get out and you miss it dreadfully. You find the only people who understand this are other newspaper types, so you hang around with them because they do not ask hard questions about why you're living this way.

Newspaper work ruins marriages, intestinal tracts and one's sense of reality. It is a treadmill of deadlines surrounded by too much coffee, too many cigarettes, half-eaten sandwiches, 12-hour days, phones that won't stop ringing and words that won't come when needed. A newsroom is the world's only torture chamber with a waiting list, an asylum run by inmates

> It is a treadmill of deadlines surrounded by too much coffee, too many cigarettes, half-eaten sandwiches, 12-hour days, phones that won't stop ringing and words that won't come when needed.

begging not to be let out into the sane world.

These thoughts are prompted by the morning-after's reflection upon one of those rare events that keeps us toiling away in the nuthouse of newspapering.

Why would anybody put up with the life journalists choose for themselves? Because, at unexpected moments, when you are close to exhausting whatever it is that keeps you going, a lightning bolt of pure joy electrifies the entire asylum, recharging egos and zapping the blues away.

So it was last Wednesday. It was 2:17 p.m. when my computer terminal, keyed in to display the latest bulletins moving on the news wires, offered a bolt from the blue in glowing green letters: Tom Knudson of The Des Moines Register had won the Pulitzer Prize for national reporting.

You tell me what the odds are that a 31-year-old kid from Council Bluffs, working out of a one-man news bureau in Iowa City, is going to win the Pulitzer for national reporting against the likes of The New York Times, The

How sweet it is! We celebrate with a stack of Pulitzer Prize cakes in the Des Moines Register newsroom with Publisher Charles Edwards (left) and Richard Gilbert, then President of the Register & Tribune Company.

Washington Post, The Wall Street Journal and the Associated Press. Whatever the odds, that's what Knudson did with his six-part series examining his startling finding that farming has become the most hazardous occupation in America.

Knudson took a mundane subject, safety and health dangers on the farm, and turned it into a compelling human saga titled "A Harvest of Harm: The Farm-Health Crisis." He did it by digging deep into the real stories of lives lost or damaged by machines that maim and kill and disease dangers that lurk in silos, grain bins, hog sheds and chemical sprays. He did it by driving down dusty gravel roads to find farmhouses where a widow or a farmer with one hand might tell a story. He did it the old-fashioned way, without a leaked document or an anonymous source, and he did it alone.

That's why I think Knudson's prize was a shared thrill for the entire Register staff. It was not a prize honoring something remote from us. It was for the journalism we understood, the journalism we do every day, the journalism that is the shared experience of all the inmates of the asylum: Drive down road, talk to people, write story, win Pulitzer. See how easy it is? Why, any one of us could do that! You don't have to talk to presidents or hide in the shadows waiting for a CIA leaker or sneak into Afghanistan. You can beat The New York Times by driving down dusty Iowa roads, talking to people!

Don't you see the energizing charge of that realization? It says that no matter where you are, no matter what your story, no matter what your age or experience or pedigree, journalism's ultimate award is there to grab, waiting only for the transparent display of individual excellence. It says a board of august authorities, gathering at Columbia University in New York City each spring, will see the brilliance of a lone reporter's light, even over this distant horizon, if it shines with the brightness of the best.

For that sweet moment of shared joy, we enthusiastically embrace this life of measured torture, asking the forgiveness of our families and praying, only for the chance to see this happen, dear God, one more time.

"WRITE WITH COMPASSION," THE OLD MAN SAID

The Des Moines Sunday Register, July 28, 1985

One of those classic cancel-my-subscription letters crossed the editor's desk last week. The letter, published today on our letters page, cited an editorial as the last straw in a string of offenses that irked an Ames reader. The editorial, written the day that President Reagan's doctors revealed he had cancer, simply expressed The Register's hope for "a complete and quick recovery for the man who leads our nation."

That was "drippy," writes William McCarthy, who says he's had enough such "sagging at the knees" on our editorial page. I suppose our coming out against the president's cancer does disappoint some readers who expect The Register to kick Reagan at least once a day, even if he's in a surgical ward. I would have ignored the letter except that it came from a college teacher at Iowa State University, and it reminded me of a voice from my college days, and a lesson that lies behind that editorial.

Dear Mr. McCarthy:

When I was a young man in college, I had the rare good fortune to study under a great man and a great journalism educator, Dean J. L. O'Sullivan of the Marquette University College of Journalism. He was an old man then, perhaps 60 or so, and those of us who were one-third his age thought him somewhat quaint in some of his views.

> But in more recent years, O'Sullivan's commandment began to loom large in my conscience as a writer and then as editor.

Think back on your own college education and try to remember one specific idea that still rings in your ears. You're lucky if even one professor ever said anything that meaningful or memorable. But J. L. O'Sullivan did, and I remember it distinctly, 25 years later.

"Write with compassion," he said. He said it fervently. "Write with compassion for your fellow human beings."

At the time, as a 20-year-old college kid eager to prove that I had the stone heart necessary to be a newspaperman, I didn't really know what to make of old Jerry O'Sullivan's "compassion" idea. I wasn't sure there was room for compassion in journalism. I knew there was plenty of room — perhaps requirement — for skepticism, for aggressiveness, for uncompromising insistence on the public's right to know. But compassion? Where did that fit in the hard-bitten code of journalism?

I never figured it out in college, and I don't think I gave it much thought in my early years in the reporter's trade. I was too busy fulfilling my ambitions, broadening my experience, "making it" in the business. Compassion wasn't on my agenda.

But in more recent years, O'Sullivan's commandment began to loom large in my conscience as a writer and then as editor. Perhaps part of it was just getting older and seeing how fate treats people unfairly, and how compassion is about all we sometimes have to offer those upon whom disaster, disease, and other ill-fortune are visited.

Perhaps it in part was a lesson learned in Iowa, where compassion seems to come naturally to most people. Perhaps it was a growing understanding on my part of how much of society sees journalists as vultures, preying on the misfortunes of others, with so little evidence of compassion. Whatever the reasons, O'Sullivan's commandment has become one important guideline in my own code of good journalism. There is a place for compassion in this business. It can coexist with skepticism, aggressive pursuit of truth and the public's right to know.

It is not a sign of weakness for a writer or an editor to develop some sensitivity to human pain and anguish, and at least to consider whether what's printed will unnecessarily add to a person's suffering. And it's no shame — though perhaps it is drippy — for an editorial writer to show, on special occasions, that some human blood flows through the hand that writes the opinions that speak for the newspaper.

So when we put aside our views of the president's policies and politics and unashamedly revealed that we had a soft spot in our heart for anyone who gets cancer, we were putting the memory of O'Sullivan's commandment into practice. If he were still teaching college today, there's no doubt he'd still be preaching that same "compassion" line. Of course, he would be considered hopelessly quaint — if not drippy.

Sincerely,

James P. Gannon

A NEWSPAPER GOES ON THE AUCTION BLOCK

The Des Moines Sunday Register, December 9, 1984

It was just a chance encounter in a hardware store, but in its odd little way, it had a telling impact on me. The man with the little boy looked at me, then asked, "Excuse me, are you James Gannon?" When I said I was, he responded: "You have a very fine newspaper. I don't understand what is going on down there with your paper, but let's hope it stays independent — for the good of Iowa."

I thanked him, and he took his little boy's hand and walked away, leaving me to ponder what he said, and what I felt at his saying it.

"I don't understand what is going on down there. . ."

What's going on is not unusual in business today. The Des Moines Register and Tribune Company is experiencing what many American businesses have experienced in this age of mergers and buy-outs — pressure from within and without to sell.

This happens when a company's underlying value is much higher than the going price of its stock. Smart people who can see the real value seek to buy it at a bargain, and they're helped by unhappy stockholders who can't see the real value and are eager to sell to the people who can. The two forces build pressure from inside and outside the company to sell.

That's why there have been at least three offers to buy this company, even though its chief executive, David Kruidenier, has insisted it's not for sale. The odd twist in this case is that one of those offers came from the second- and third-ranking executives of the Register and Tribune, in association with Dow Jones & Co. and two other Iowans. This is sort of like having your two older brothers and a large bank trying to buy your mom and dad's house, even though your parents don't want to move. You want to run to the basement and hide.

". . . Let's hope it stays independent...."

At the top left corner of this page we declare ourselves "an independent newspaper." That independence is a many-splendored thing, and our prize asset. We are independent of any political party, government power, special-interest group or economic interest. At times we even bite the hands that feed us — when we publish news articles or editorial commentary unfavorable to advertisers — and we often irritate friends.

But, like the man in the hardware store, Iowans generally understand the need and value of such independence in a newspaper, and I doubt they'd want to lose it any more than I would.

This is the age of newspaper chains and media conglomerates. Some of those corporations publish excellent papers — journalistically independent, courageous and public-spirited. Others publish weak, timid, or irresponsible embarrassments to journalism. A newspaper is only as good as its publisher's commitment to quality, integrity and independence. Such has been the hall-mark of The Register for 80-plus years under Cowles family ownership. Would it continue under other ownership? Perhaps. Perhaps not.

"... For the good of Iowa."

The man in the hardware store managed to capture, in a sentence, what I have been trying to define and articulate as the special role of The Register in the life of this state. I think that role is unlike anything else in American jour-nalism today — a symbiotic relationship in which The Register both influences and reflects the character of Iowa, and vice versa.

For the past couple of years, I have given a set speech to many audiences trying to articulate this notion. These are the key thoughts:

The Register is the last of the truly statewide newspapers in America. It is not a Des Moines paper, it is an Iowa paper. It is the only paper in the country that treats a whole state as its hometown. The idea that is the driving force of The Register is that Iowa needs and deserves one outstanding statewide news-paper that serves as Iowa's common source of information, its public forum of ideas and opinion, and its main marketplace of advertising. Its role helps unify and motivate the state as a civic entity, as a culture, and as a marketplace.

168

Iowa is what it is partly because of The Register — and The Register is what it is because of Iowa's special character.

Tomorrow, 10 people will meet in Des Moines to decide the future for The Register. I hope these company directors understand that all of us, from the man in the hardware store to the editors on the news floor, are counting on their vision, wisdom and courage to do what's right to preserve a proud tradition.

What happened next was not pretty to watch nor fun to participate in. The company's board of directors put The Register and other assets up for sale, inviting all bidders. They swarmed in like bees: Hearst Corp., The Washington Post Company, The Chicago Tribune, Gannett Company and others. On July 1, 1985, The Register was taken over by Gannett, publisher of USA Today and about 100 other U.S. newspapers. I remained as editor under Gannett for the next three-and-one-half years.

My Farewell to Journalism: A Lament on Trends in the News

The Detroit News, July 24, 1994

At the end of this month, I will leave daily journalism after 33 years as a reporter, columnist, bureau chief and editor to begin work on a book.

The news business has been good to me, and I leave it with gratitude, a sense of accomplishment and no regrets. I am not going away mad. But I am going away concerned about trends in the news business that I believe are harmful to the health of quality journalism.

There are powerful forces reshaping the news media. In an age when newspaper readership is declining and the audiences for network news programs are falling, owners and managers of media properties are rightfully concerned about their future. In a desperate search for audience, they are increasingly substituting entertainment values for news values.

As a result, we are substituting sensation for significance and style for substance. Too often, we are combining the attributes of the tabloid newspaper and the TV talk show into a lowest-common-denominator form of journalism that cheapens our products and trivializes our professional purpose.

> **We have a new kind of food chain in journalism: if a sensational story appears anywhere, it appears everywhere.**

The new media reality is this: If a story can get into the tabloids or on the talk shows, it can and will get into the mainstream press, including daily newspapers. The new rules of the media are simple: There are no rules.

A good example: After a Florida tabloid

printed the name of the woman allegedly raped by Ted Kennedy's nephew, William Kennedy Smith, NBC Television decided to name her, despite its general policy against identifying rape victims. Since NBC did, the New York Times decided it should name the woman, since her identity had become public knowledge. Thus do tabloid standards become the standards of even the New York Times. (The Detroit News also named the woman after her identity was revealed).

There are so many similar examples that the triumph of tabloidism is nearly complete.

We have a new kind of food chain in journalism: if a sensational story appears anywhere, it appears everywhere. We're like fish in the ocean, feeding off each other. If the bottom-suckers find something down there in the muck, they dredge it up and we gobble up their story because the whole hungry school of media fish is right there in feeding frenzy with us.

I am not saying all is lost for American journalism. There is still plenty of outstanding daily newspapering being done. So we have not lost our souls. But there is a struggle under way for the soul of journalism — and many respected veterans of our business believe the struggle is being lost. I believe that what has happened to television, where the battle is all but lost, is spilling over into newspapers.

The other day I saw an interview with Paul Duke, who for 20 years was moderator of Washington Week in Review. Under Duke, that PBS program was a holdout against the trend of shouting-head journalism. It was an intelligent, lively, dignified discussion of serious news topics — unlike the new generation of shows, such as The McLaughlin Group, that turn journalists into buffoons and reduce all issues to quips and shouted opinions.

In the interview, Duke was asked why he said that broadcast journalism had become "a slum." He replied:

"Because there has been an across-the-board deterioration of standards.... We used to do a lot of hour-long documentaries. The networks almost never do that any more. Instead they have new magazine type programs filled with celebrity interviews and sob stories. All this is ratings driven. Profits are driven by ratings.... Watch the Donahue-type shows some time. They are no longer just television talk shows. They're more like freak shows. We're getting checkout-counter journalism. That stuff is getting into the mainstream press, and I hate to see it."

As Duke suggests, the seepage of checkout-counter journalism into mainstream newspapers is clear to see.

Remember last year's media frenzy over the story of Lorena and John Bobbitt? (It was a lurid story of a wife who cut off her husband's penis.) Sure it was a lurid and fascinating tale, worthy of a thousand bad jokes. But the media exploited it shamelessly, turning it into more than what it was — a random act of violence. We made it a touchstone of our times, a moral tale of modem man and woman, told in endless chapters.

It's the same with so many stories: Gennifer Flowers and her claims of an affair with Bill Clinton; Michael Jackson and his fun with little boys. This used to be the stuff of the National Enquirer, but it's Page One now, everywhere. Do Madonna's foul-mouthed antics on late-night TV belong on Page One of a serious newspaper? I don't think so, but some editors do.

Newspaper editors are taking too many cues from television. Just because a topic is a ratings success on Oprah or Donahue doesn't mean it belongs on Page One of a serious newspaper. Newspapers make a mistake trying to compete with television for sensation and titillation. TV can do that better than we can.

We can do serious reporting on complex subjects better than TV can. We can provide readers more detail, more useful information, more insight, and more value for their nickel than TV can. We can't out-trash TV, and we shouldn't try.

We seriously underestimate our readers. I believe they are more interested in hard news and helpful information than many editors think they are. They care more about everyday problems of ordinary people than about the bizarre problems of celebrities. And they look to newspapers for this kind of helpful, serious news that they don't get on television — and they are disappointed when they find a second-day version of TV titillation in their newspapers.

Too many newspapers are cheating their readers and cheapening their product in other ways — by squeezing down news space and reducing staffs. Gene Roberts, the legendary editor of the Philadelphia Inquirer who has just become managing editor of The New York Times, made this point in a recent speech. Recalling his early days as a reporter in Goldsboro, N.C., Roberts said, "I learned never to underestimate readers." They will chuckle at trivia stories, Roberts said, "but they expect depth when stories arise that are important to them. I learned that if tobacco prices were going up or down there was no limit to their demand for detail."

"I wish some of today's publishing executives had been out in the tobacco rows with me," Roberts continued. "They would have learned that formula and slickness cannot substitute for substantive news coverage.... Today, as competition diminishes and disappears, many newspapers seem to be in a race to see which can be the most shortsighted and superficial. We are relying too much, far too much, on weather maps, charts, graphs, briefs and color."

I think Roberts is right. Don't get me wrong — I think color, better graphics, quick summaries of stories and other new devices of design are real improvements in newspapers — as supplements to depth reporting. But too often now, they are substitutes for depth reporting. Better design is fine, but it is no substitute for content. Detailed reporting and fine writing are the essence of content, and they have fallen too low on the priority lists at many newspapers.

The story, in many cases, has become incidental to the design. Too often, the story is whatever car be squeezed into a tight news hole after the designers reserve space for headlines, pictures, graphics, summaries, pullout quotes, white space and reader call-in boxes — if there is any space left at all.

As Roberts warned: "We introduced many of these devices in order to reach out to marginal readers and nonreaders. This was good. But when we started cutting back on substance, we put serious, devoted readers at risk by becoming less essential to them. And this was, and is, a very bad trade-off. I think, quite simply, that we are imperiling newspapers in the name of saving them."

As I wind up a third of a century in this business, that's what worries me. I hope I'm wrong. I hope that newspapers will prosper in the future. But I don't think they will unless more editors heed Gene Roberts and remember that content is the thing — and our business is news, not entertainment.

A Life in Print: From Camelot to Clinton, He wrote history while it was still news

The Detroit News, July 31, 1994

In the summer of 1961, a 22-year-old journalism college graduate walked into the Chicago bureau of The Wall Street Journal to take his first full-time job as a reporter. He was young, green and scared.

He was given a desk, an old Royal typewriter, and a warning from his boss: "We operate on a sink-or-swim policy here. You have six months to show that you can do the job." Swimming furiously, he barely survived the trial period. He wondered in those days if he would last long as a journalist. He had his doubts.

That was the beginning of a 33-year journey that ends this month. The young reporter grew in ability and confidence, rising through a series of jobs to fulfill his career dreams. He covered the White House, Congress, national political campaigns. He became the editor of a major daily newspaper, a columnist, a Washington bureau chief. He witnessed and wrote history while it was still news.

I was that young reporter starting out, green and hopeful, in the Camelot days of John F. Kennedy's presidency. For a third of a century, I've had one of the best seats in the house to watch American history unfold, and to help tell the story. I've watched the country — and the news business — change profoundly from the early Sixties to the mid-Nineties.

It should be hard to walk away from this, but it isn't. An inner voice says it's time to go. But not before trying, this one last time, to put it all in some perspective — for myself if nobody else. So indulge me, if you will, in this farewell memoir.

174

THE SIXTIES

Chicago in the 1960s was robust and feisty, a great news town. "Da Mare," Richard Daley (the original Daley) was in charge — totally. Four daily newspapers competed fiercely. It was still the city of big shoulders, hog slaughterer to the world, muscular home of steel mills and rail yards.

But the old industrial order was dying. I was assigned to cover agriculture and agribusiness. The huge packing plants near the stockyards were closing down and moving closer to the cattle and hogs in Iowa, Nebraska, Kansas. Good paying jobs that supported families — many of them black families — disappeared with them. The old steel mills on the South Side were sliding into obsolescence, unable to compete with imported steel.

I reported on these dinosaurs of American industry without understanding how profoundly the U.S. economy and its cities were being changed, or the disastrous impact that would have in coming decades on blue-collar workers and the black family.

I helped cover the railroad industry, also sliding into decline. I rode storied passenger trains — soon to disappear — on assignments. Santa Fe's Super Chief took me to Dodge City, Kansas, to profile wheat farmer Jack McNair. He opened his life — even his tax returns — to a reporter from Chicago, in hopes that urban readers might understand the hard work, high risk, and uncertain rewards of modern farming. He trusted me. I admired him and his kind.

The foreboding sense that things were coming unstuck in America started with Kennedy's assassination on November 22, 1963. There's no way to overstate the impact that one event had on this country. A madman's act snuffed out hope and dreams, prompting national anguish and doubts. And after Dallas, the Sixties went to hell.

I agitated for The Wall Street Journal to send me to Washington, which I saw then as the news Mecca. I arrived in 1966 as Lyndon Johnson was escalating the war in Vietnam. My job was to cover labor. It was the era of labor's giants — George Meany and Jimmy Hoffa and Walter Reuther. I wrote of strikes, labor negotiations and union corruption.

Then came the nightmare year, 1968. As more than 500 American soldiers died in Vietnam every week, Lyndon Johnson announced he would not seek another term as president. A gunman assassinated Martin Luther King Jr. in

Memphis, triggering race riots nationwide. Soon Robert F. Kennedy was killed in Los Angeles. All our heroes lay murdered.

Then came my introduction to covering national politics: the Democratic convention in Chicago in 1968. What a baptism! The city was engulfed in street riots by antiwar protesters, who were brutally attacked by Daley's police. I remember standing in the lobby of the Conrad Hilton Hotel, full of bloodied heads and the smell of tear gas, and thinking that The Revolution had come.

Whenever I am tempted to think this country is coming apart, I remember 1968. Any nation that can survive and rebound from such chaos and despair has amazing resiliency. The Sixties tested America's stability. We survived.

THE SEVENTIES

In mid-1969, the Journal named me its bureau chief in Pittsburgh. The job opened a window on the global economy then emerging. Japan, Taiwan and other foreign competitors were eating the American steel industry's lunch. Jobs evaporated, mills closed, steel companies merged or died. The Steelworkers' Union shrank to half its former size. This was the story from Pittsburgh.

But my heart was back in Washington, and after three years I asked the Journal to send me back. They did — assigning me to cover Richard Nixon's White House. Only later did I understand it was not an honor, but punishment. I'll never forget what Alan Otten, then Washington Bureau Chief, told me about Nixon when I took the job: "This is an evil man." At the time, Otten's view struck me as extreme. Before long, events proved he was right.

Covering Nixon's White House was the worst reporting job I ever had. Nixon hated the press, and his staff reflected that. Only a few — Pat Buchanan, Bill Safire, John Ehrlichman — would talk to me. Sources were scarce, and control of the White House press corps was tight. My daily routine was being lied to by Ron Ziegler, Nixon's mouthpiece.

Two metro reporters from the Washington Post were shaming the White House press corps on the only story that mattered, the Watergate break-in. They eventually would bring down Nixon, while we watched. It wasn't fun.

In 1973, I escaped to the economic-policy beat, covering the Treasury, the Federal Reserve, and other economic agencies. Nixon had imposed wage and price controls, a straitjacket for the economy that had bureaucrats policing the price of paper clips. Inevitably, shortages, black markets and other economic distortions occurred, proving that government can damage economies but can't control them.

Amid the Watergate crisis, Treasury Secretary William Simon offered me the job of Assistant Secretary for Public Affairs. Big office. Nice Salary. Insider's look at government. Working for Nixon. No thanks, I said. Best career decision I ever made.

Gerald Ford's presidency brought calm to Washington and economic recession to the nation. Ford's economic advisers, including the esteemed Alan Greenspan, now chairman of the Fed, thought inflation was the real threat to the economy then. (I still have my Ford WIN button — Whip Inflation Now.) None of them foresaw the deep recession coming. Lesson: The best economists' forecasts, even Greenspan's, have the same value as astrology.

Eager to cover politics again, I was assigned to the 1976 presidential campaign. Jimmy Carter was a political phenomenon — best campaigner I ever saw — and offered promise of bringing together the nation, North and South, black and white, after years of turmoil and crisis. But his presidency was overtaken by forces beyond his control — the energy crisis, inflation, the Iran hostage nightmare. A fed-up nation soon turned to a genial actor, Ronald Reagan, for salvation.

The Seventies undermined Americans' trust in government and their confidence about the future.

THE EIGHTIES

My Eighties decade started early, in mid-1978, when I left Washington and The Wall Street Journal to become executive editor of The Des Moines Register and Tribune in Iowa. The next 10 years were filled with great highs and lows.

Your view of the Eighties depends on where you watched that decade from. If you were a Wall Street broker, they were great years. If you were a factory worker, they were not. If you were an Iowa farmer, they were a disaster — a fact that greatly shaped life in Iowa generally.

The agricultural economy had prospered in the Seventies. Farmers had high incomes, access to easy credit and incentives to expand by buying land, machinery and livestock with borrowed money. When the inflation bubble of the 1970s burst and farmland prices collapsed, the whole house of cards came down — farmers went bankrupt, banks went belly up, small towns suffered — and so did Iowa newspapers, which depend on them all for advertising.

So I found myself in charge of a great newspaper struggling with a depression. There were wonderful moments — we won three Pulitzer Prizes during my years there — and awful ones, including a decision (not mine) to kill our afternoon daily, the Des Moines Tribune. My part of the killing — no gentler word suffices — was to pare the combined news staffs of the two papers from about 240 persons to 180. A few quit or retired, but I had to lay off about 50 reporters, photographers, copy editors and others — none of whom deserved to lose a job.

The nadir of my newspaper career: I am sitting in an executive office calling in employees one by one, telling them they are out of a job. It is like a serial murder. They react with varying degrees of shock, anger, grief. One of those I had to lay off was a photographer named George Ceolla. We had been college classmates and friends since age 18. When I told him, he looked at me and said: "Who would have thought, Jim, that it would come to this?" Then we wept together.

I learned a lot about management in the Eighties, and about newspaper economics and newspaper readers. Mostly, I learned that management isn't much fun, newspaper economics can be brutal, and readers were getting scarcer. By the end of the decade, The Register had been sold to the Gannett Company. Family or local ownership of newspapers grew rare in the Eighties as corporate ownership spread.

Despite its stresses, Iowa was a good place to spend the Eighties. If it was the Decade of Greed, it didn't seem so there — people were into survival, not getting rich. If it was the "me decade," you couldn't tell that in Iowa — people genuinely care and treat each other as neighbors.

We also conducted a great political circus in Iowa in the Eighties. In 1980, 1984 and 1988, the national presidential campaign began in Iowa, and I sponsored and moderated political debates among the contenders. It was like being ringmaster. The candidates jumped through Iowa's hoops, while I cracked the whip. Now that was fun.

I left Iowa at the end of 1988 to return to Washington and writing — as

Washington Bureau Chief and columnist for The Detroit News. I wouldn't trade my experience in Iowa for a million bucks—nor do it again for a million.

THE NINETIES

My third tour of duty in Washington began as George H.W. Bush became president. I soon realized how much Washington had changed in my decade away. The politics was meaner, the journalism more confrontational and television-dominated, and the public's belief in government as problem-solver was dissipated.

The Reagan years left the federal government hamstrung by debt, which ballooned from $829 million in 1979 to $3.2 trillion in 1990. The debt burden, combined with Bush's bankruptcy of ideas (he as a man who simply wanted to be president, not do anything with it) robbed Washington of the resources and the will to tackle serious domestic problems.

The city no longer seemed the vital news center of the nation. Washington was a mere spectator in the greatest story in years, the collapse of communism and the end of the Cold War. And on the home front, the real innovators in government — on welfare, crime, social policy — were the state governors. Out of money and ideas, but bristling with partisanship, Washington in the

President Bill Clinton perfectly fit the 1990s—smart, hip and fast-moving, a glittering bubble waiting to burst.

Bush years became the story of gridlock — about an interesting to cover as a scoreless soccer game between two teams you dislike.

The presidential campaign of 1992 promised some diversion, and the possibility of real change. But somewhere along the campaign trail — I think it was in New York covering Bill Clinton on the Phil Donohue show talking about his sex life — I realized that presidential campaigns, too, had become part of the Nineties trend to turn everything into televised entertainment. I knew it was the last presidential campaign I wanted to cover.

Sometime before the election, I decided if Bush were re-elected, I would quit — not in protest, but in despair at the thought of four more years of watching paint dry. But Clinton's victory persuaded me to hang around a while to see what happens when one party controls both the White House and Congress.

Oddly enough, not much happens. There's a marginal increase in activity in Washington, some sharpening of focus (Clinton does have an agenda), but real change comes slowly, if at all. Washington is a city pushed and pulled in so many conflicting directions by so many special interests, that any forward momentum is almost accidental.

So it seems to me that the Nineties are the decade of declining expectations. The public is cynical, politicians are too scared to make decisions, and the news media are heavily into entertainment. Political discourse has degenerated into Rush Limbaugh vs. the MTV president.

But real life isn't a talk show. Real life—out there beyond the Beltway—is about families and neighborhoods and communities trying hard to hold together in a world full of forces trying to tear them apart. And it seems to me that the solutions to the nation's big problems—crime, poor schools, dissolving families, and the decay of both virtue and responsibility—are out there too.

If the big problems are to be solved, they will be solved not in Washington but out there, at home in America, where the real people are. The promise of the Nineties, I think, is that more and more Americans are realizing that truth, and will act on it in their own families and communities. It's our best hope.

With this column, I bowed out of daily newspaper journalism. It had been a wonderful ride, more than I could have ever hoped for.

8

RETIREMENT

"Our community is called Scrabble, a tiny crossroads at the foot of Bessie Bell Mountain. It sounds like a make-believe place, but it's real. The key landmarks of Scrabble are the Mount Lebanon Baptist Church (founded 1833), Dennis's Store, and the Scrabble dump, which sits on the site of a closed, two-room schoolhouse. We live just down the dead end road from Dennis's Store, along Blackwater Creek, in the shadow of two giant oak trees. Thus the name of our place, Blackwater Oaks."

RETIRING 75 MILES AND 75 YEARS AWAY FROM WASHINGTON DC

Gannett News Service, September 1994

After 33 years in the news business, I retired from The Detroit News in August 1994. I agreed to continue writing a weekly column of commentary for the Gannett News Service, the Gannett Co.'s wire service for its 100-plus newspapers. This is the first of these columns of a retiree.

SCRABBLE, VA.—After a dozen years of dreaming, we are actually moving to Blackwater Oaks, the rural retreat in the foothills of the Blue Ridge Mountains that will be our new home. It is 27 acres of God's handiwork tucked away in a woods on a dead-end gravel road. To get there, you turn off the road on to a private lane that winds through towering oak, hickory and pine trees. The lane skirts the edge of our neighbor's pasture and wanders down the hill to an open knoll where we are building our dream house overlooking a grassy meadow.

We bought the land 12 years ago with the idea that someday, we would live here. Suddenly, Someday has arrived. At the end of this month, we will vacate our home in the suburbs of Washington and settle in Rappahannock County, Virginia — a place that progress forgot, thank God.

Rappahannock County is a rare gem of rural beauty that lies just outside the lay-

In the entire county, there is not a single fast-food restaurant, nor a supermarket, and of course nothing even approaching a shopping mall.

ers of cheap costume jewelry that make up the suburban necklace around Washington. One of Rappahannock's best known residents, Gene McCarthy — the former Minnesota senator and frequent presidential candidate — has written that the county is "75 miles and 75 years away from Washington, D.C."

McCarthy is right. The county is a time capsule preserving the way America once was. It is an agricultural county where cows outnumber people and the villages have names like Flint Hill, Slate Mills, and Viewtown. The 1990 census found 6,622 residents of the county, or about 19 per square mile. The population peaked before the Civil War at about 9,700 in 1850 and has declined pretty steadily since then — which is just fine with most folks here.

In the entire county, there is not a single fast-food restaurant, nor a supermarket, and of course nothing even approaching a shopping mall. But there are 50 or so churches — mostly Baptists of various persuasions — several good country stores, a farm co-op, a half-dozen good restaurants and one weekly newspaper, The Rappahannock News, circulation 2,950.

Our community is called Scrabble, a tiny crossroads at the foot of Bessie Bell Mountain. It sounds like a make-believe place, but it's real. The key landmarks of Scrabble are the Mount Lebanon Baptist Church (founded 1833), Dennis's Store, and the Scrabble dump, which sits on the site of a closed, two-room schoolhouse. We live just down the dead end road from Dennis's Store, along Blackwater Creek, in the shadow of two giant oak trees. Thus the name of our place, Blackwater Oaks.

Rappahannock County, in short, is Way Beyond the Beltway. It is so far removed from Washington's inside-the-Beltway mentality that it is the perfect escape for a middle-aged columnist who has come to believe that the national capital is gripped by some collective insanity. After years of observing Washington from the inside, I wanted to find some vantage point safely beyond the reach of the capital's self-deluding perspective. The move to Rappahannock is both a chance to create a simpler, rural lifestyle and a reaching for a new perspective as a writer — both as a columnist and aspiring novelist.

This, then, is a column reborn. These weekly essays will deal with the mundane and the sublime, but less often than before with the ridiculous. Which is to say, I hope to write more about real life, and less about politics. I aim to write about ordinary things that are important things — family, friends, faith, community, the land, work, play — the stuff of life. From time to time, I hope to have something worth saying on issues as diverse as religion and American culture, the performance of the media and the lessons of history. Once in a while, I suppose, I will succumb to the temptation to comment on something going on in Washington, but I will do so from a safe distance from the capital's spin doctors and the insanity virus.

Our move to the country is in once sense an escape, but in another sense a chance to reconnect with real life. I hope that these columns will reflect the best of both those aspirations.

Books, books, books:
What to do with them all?

Gannett News Service, September 1994

Scrabble, Va. – The new house we are building here at the place we call Blackwater Oaks has a library. It is both a luxury and a necessity. Books are a weakness of mine. I hate to pass a bookstore without going in. Over the years, this has added up to a sizable problem that required either that I open a used bookstore or build a library in our new home.

The bookstore option was tempting but impractical. So the house has a not-quite-finished room with a high ceiling, a stone fireplace, walnut-paneled walls made from trees cut from our land, and a huge window overlooking the pasture. Filled with books, it will be a reader's dream. My wife fears that I will retreat to the library and never come out. It's a possibility.

But right now, the dream is closer to a nightmare. The books have to be moved from our old house to the new one. This is inordinately time-consuming; for it requires a careful consideration of the merits of each book and the likelihood that I might want to actually read it some day.

I swore before the process began that I would ruthlessly weed out my collection. I dreamed of the riches I would reap by taking the discards to a used bookstore. Think of all the books I'll be able to buy when I sell these, I thought. Ha.

> **My wife fears that I will retreat to the library and never come out. It's a possibility.**

If you have lots of books you don't want, I have this advice: give them away. Don't even bother trying to sell them, if you consider your time worth more than 98 cents an hour.

There was, for example, the question of whether to keep Will and Ariel Durant's 10-volume history of Western civilization. I've owned it for years without cracking one of the volumes. But it will look great in the library — the mark of an educated man.

On the other end of the scale, there was "Know your Cairn Terrier," a handbook for owners of the breed. I once had a Cairn named Tricky Dick (guess which president I was covering when I bought him?) and someday I might get another. Must keep.

So it went, book by book. Soon I had a truckload of books to keep, and a car-load of books to sell. I packed the discards — novels, histories, biographies, books on politics, government, travel and more — into the car. I was off to cash in.

I lugged three or four heavy boxes into the first used bookstore I visited. The owner pawed through them, grunting occasionally. "Can't use any of these — I'm overstocked as it is. Got anything else?" Shocked, I told him I had a box of old magazines in the car.. He went out to look them over. Picking up two old copies of Life, he said, "I can give you $1.50 for these." I took it and left.

I tried two other used booksellers. One bought books only by the box, at $6 a box. From my several boxes, she selected just over a box worth. I left with $7. At the third store, they bought by the book, and took about three dozen carefully selected volumes for the princely sum of $23.

Several days' work had produced $31.50 and a feeling I'd sold my prizes for a pittance. In my car, I still had two boxes of books that nobody wanted. As I drove to our new home, I stopped at the Scrabble dump, where I often see scavengers picking over other people's discards. I left my old books there. Later that day, when I drove by there again, the books were gone. Somehow, that gave me more satisfaction than my attempts to sell them.

Somebody out here might actually be reading them. On the other hand, chances are the finder is trying to cash in at the local used bookstore. Ha.

The irony here is that, four years after I wrote this column, I actually did open a bookstore. My wife Joan and I operated the Old Sperryville Bookshop in a former Episcopal Church in Sperryville, Virginia, for five years before selling the business in 2003.

EXCUSE ME, WHILE I SLIP AWAY INTO HISTORY

Gannett News Service, July 1995

Scrabble, Va. — Sometimes I think I was born into the wrong century. As an avid reader of American history, I find the story of our country's past so compelling that I deeply regret not having been a part of it.

The history of America is a story of ordinary people rising to heroic deeds, again and again, from the American Revolution through World War II. For some reason, the fifty-plus years of American history that I have lived through somehow seem less exciting, less noble, less heroic than the roughly two centuries that preceded them.

I am not sure whether this is because we tend to romanticize the past or whether it reflects a real change in the American people and the American experience. Surely, to some degree, the history we read, with heroic figures such as Jefferson, Lincoln, Lee, the Roosevelts and Eisenhower has a grandeur that the history that we live cannot match. So perception is part of the problem.

But I believe that reality is part of the problem, too. That is, I believe that the American people of these last years of the 20th Century are fundamentally different from their ancestors of 200, 100 or even 50 years ago. Our recent history seems less noble, less heroic than our older history because there is an objective decline in nobility and heroism in the American people.

> I have spent more time reading about Robert E. Lee than about Bill Clinton.

Certainly heroic leaders are hard to find in modern America. In the past year, as a part-time columnist and an aspiring writer of Civil

War history, I have spent more time reading about Robert E. Lee than about Bill Clinton. I find Lee infinitely more interesting, infinitely more admirable. Newt Gingrich, the most interesting politician in America today, is no Lincoln—some would say he's not even a Ford (Henry or Jerry, take your pick.).

But we can't just blame lack of leaders. Heroic followers are harder to find, too. When you think about it, it wasn't heroic leaders that made this country great, it was a collective quality of heroic followership. Often the common people of this nation have responded to crisis with sacrifice and dedication, willingly risking life, fortune and their very futures to secure the blessings of liberty for their children. This is what I find the compelling quality of American history, and the ingredient that seems in such doubtful supply today.

I read with wonder, for example, of the response of ordinary people, North and South, to the outbreak of the Civil War. There was a compelling sense of duty to country, in both sections, which drew most adult males to willingly fight the bloodiest, most costly war in American history. I read with awe of their endurance of those four years of suffering and devastation dwarfing anything Americans have endured since.

That sense of duty and honor that compelled such heroic followership has been part of the American story since the Revolution. Duty and honor seem such quaint, old-fashioned concepts in this era of rights and privileges, of instant gratification and entitlement. Today's American is much more likely to think of what his country owes him, rather than what he owes his country.

My Irish immigrant ancestors did not come to America looking for Food Stamps. They dug canals, built railroads, carved farms out of the Frontier wilderness. When crisis called, they joined the Union and Confederate armies, and in places named Fredericksburg, Gettysburg and the Wilderness, they fought and killed each other, because they believed it was their duty to do so, and their honor required it.

As I have continued my Civil War research in the past year, the story of the 1860s has become so compelling and inspiring that I have found it much harder to concentrate on the story of the 1990s. My head and heart are in another century, and I am out of tune with my times. The present players on the stage — Bill and Hillary, Newt, O.J., and the rest — cast such small shadows compared to those engraved on history's pages.

All of which, I suppose, is an elaborate explanation for my decision to concentrate on the past rather than the present. I have found it difficult to keep up with what's going on in the 1990s while striving to understand the 1860s. The 1860s have won. With this farewell, I intend to discontinue my weekly commentaries on our times, to focus my mind and work on the century I find more compelling.

I wish to thank the many readers who have cared enough about one of these columns to write to me, whether with praise or complaint. My only regret in discontinuing the column is the breaking of a bond with such readers. Perhaps, some day, I will try to renew it. For now, please excuse me, while I disappear into history.

The result of three years of Civil War research and writing was my book "Irish Rebels, Confederate Tigers: A History of the 6th Louisiana Volunteers," published in 1998, which documented the story of a regiment of fighting Irishmen from Louisiana in Robert E. Lee's Army of Northern Virginia.

KERRY'S CATHOLICISM: CHECKED AT THE DOOR

USA Today, June 2, 2004

Author's Note: A political junkie never retires. During the 2004 election campaign, I returned to writing political commentary—as USA Today published several of my pieces, including the four reprinted here.

When John F. Kennedy ran for president in 1960, I was a college senior at Marquette University, a Catholic Jesuit college in Milwaukee. I had just turned 21, eligible to vote for the first time. As a young Catholic, I was proud that a man who shared my faith could run for the highest office in the land, so I looked forward to casting my first presidential vote for JFK.

I had heard my father's stories about Al Smith, the Democratic nominee for president in 1928, who had lost to Herbert Hoover in a campaign marked by widespread anti-Catholic bigotry aimed at Smith's religious heritage. My father was bitter about Smith's defeat and never voted Democratic again.

Kennedy's victory in 1960 over Vice President Nixon seemed to smash the political barrier to the Oval Office for Catholics, and we rejoiced. The fact that Kennedy virtually had to promise to keep his religious beliefs in a lockbox for four years, to overcome fears that the pope would be calling the shots, was a concession we could understand and forgive.

Now, 44 years later, another Catholic is about to become the Democratic nominee for president. I wish I could be as proud and enthusiastic about that as I was in 1960. Instead, I am embarrassed. Given his beliefs and his voting record, I wish John Kerry professed another religious faith or none at all. I would rather have an agnostic or an atheist in the White House than a person who proclaims himself a Catholic but tosses overboard those parts of Catholic doctrine that are politically inconvenient.

The liberal Massachusetts senator has consistently disregarded the church's teaching on the sacredness of human life by voting against any restriction on abortion, even the termination of a nearly completed pregnancy known as partial-birth abortion. He not only has voted to support abortion rights at every opportunity but he also has proudly proclaimed his stance in speeches to Democratic pro-choice groups such as NARAL. Kerry is not in the least way embarrassed by his pro-abortion stance. I am, and I believe many Catholics are, too.

I realize that many Catholics disagree with the church's teaching on abortion, homosexuality, capital punishment and other issues. Polls show American Catholics are about as deeply divided on the issue of abortion as is the general public. Exit polls taken in the 2000 election showed Catholic voters split 50% in favor of pro-choice Democrat Al Gore to 47% for pro-life Republican George W. Bush. Clearly, the pope and bishops do not dictate how U.S. Catholics vote.

But Kerry's rise to the pinnacle of American politics, with his well-advertised Catholic label, raises the stakes in this struggle for the hearts and minds of Catholic voters. Can American bishops ignore the fact that his voting record on basic moral issues defies church teaching? Can Catholics who embrace the church's teaching accept as our leader a man who so easily abandons Catholic beliefs? Kerry is carrying our flag, but he is dragging it on the ground.

Kerry rationalizes his position on abortion with the well-worn excuse used for years by Catholic politicians who find their faith's teaching inconvenient. He professes to be personally opposed to abortion as an article of faith but says it is not appropriate for a member of Congress to legislate personal religious beliefs. This position is tired and intellectually dishonest.

As he has done on so many issues, Kerry is trying to have it both ways on abortion — consistently voting as a reliable supporter of the powerful abortion-rights lobby of the Democratic Party while professing a personal belief that is consistent with his faith and supposedly comforting to Catholic voters.

He does the same kind of waffling on another issue important to the Catholic faith — the controversy over same-sex marriages. Kerry has said he opposes gay marriages, but when given an opportunity to cast a vote to support that claim, he voted against the Defense of Marriage Act, which Congress approved by large margins and was signed by Democratic President Clinton.

As a Catholic who takes the church's positions on abortion and same-sex marriage seriously, I wonder how Kerry can toss aside these "personal beliefs" so easily. Kerry seems to wear his Catholicism like a sports coat that he puts on for Sunday Mass but takes off when going to work. I don't trust a man whose supposedly deep inner convictions can be checked in the cloakroom of the Senate chamber, or cast aside at the door of the Oval Office.

Kerry does not find it inappropriate to vote in accord with Catholic teaching on other issues. He is generally opposed to capital punishment, as is the church. If it is inappropriate to vote his faith-based view on abortion, why is it appropriate to vote as the pope would on the death penalty? How about the church's social teaching on subjects such as every worker's right to a living wage? Would Kerry hesitate to vote for a raise in the minimum wage because someone might think he's voting his religious belief? Not on your life.

Kerry is consistent in voting in line with liberal Democratic orthodoxy: against abortion restrictions, against restrictions on gay marriage, against capital punishment and for social welfare legislation such as the minimum wage. This is his true religion, based on his voting record.

John Kennedy didn't face this dilemma. He lived and died before Roe vs. Wade, before the idea of gay marriage, before the Democratic Party became a hostile environment for devout Catholics who won't check their beliefs at the door. John Kerry has made his choice on these matters. He is not one of us. I wish he would stop pretending that he is.

In the 2004 election, Catholic John Kerry lost the majority of the U.S. Catholic vote to the Protestant, pro-life president, George W. Bush. According to exit polls, the usually Democratic Catholic vote split 52% for Bush to 47% for Kerry — a sharp contrast to the estimated 78% Catholic vote for John Kennedy in 1960.

An Open Letter to Vice President Cheney

USA Today, June 21, 2004

Dear Mr. Vice President:

I am writing to you as a long-time admirer. Ever since you rose to prominence 30 years ago — when you became chief of staff to President Gerald Ford and I was a Wall Street Journal reporter covering economic policy in the Ford administration — you seemed to embody the qualities needed at the right hand of the president. Your competence, calmness amid crisis and absolute devotion to duty were obvious then, as now.

For nearly four years now, you have been a loyal and hard-working partner in the presidency of George W. Bush. Your experience, steadiness and character surely have given the president strength in these difficult times. I believe you have always considered first what is best for the president, and only secondly what is best for Dick Cheney

That question arises now in this election year. Forgive me for suggesting that self-sacrifice may be the greatest service you can render to President Bush in what promises to be a closely contested election. You must ask yourself now if your continued presence by his side will offer strength or weakness to the Republican ticket in November, and what it will mean for GOP prospects in the future.

Nobody knows better than you do that you have become a lightning rod for criticism, and a favorite target for your party's political opponents. Fair or not, it is simply too easy to paint Dick Cheney as a tool of the oil industry, a too-eager advocate of war in Iraq and a too-gullible supporter of the now-disgraced Ahmad Chalabi, who fed the Bush administration false intelligence on Iraq. Your former company, Halliburton, is a political albatross around your neck, weighing down not only you but also President Bush.

Moreover, given your history of health problems, you do not offer the Republicans what they need for 2008 and beyond — a president in training. After November, the party will need to think beyond the presidency of Bush, even if he is re-elected. Inaugurating a vice president next January who could step up to lead the party in 2008 would be a great asset for the GOP.

You know that Bush's sense of loyalty means he would never ask you to step aside. The move would have to be yours. You would have to convince the president that your stepping aside is necessary to secure a second Bush term to pursue the agenda you both share.

The nation is at war again, this time against the elusive enemy called international terrorism. In previous times of war, two great American presidents have found it necessary or desirable to change vice presidents in a re-election year.

In 1864, as the Civil War raged on, Abraham Lincoln let the Republican Party convention choose a Southern Democrat, Andrew Johnson, to replace Vice President Hannibal Hamlin on a national unity ticket. In 1944, in the midst of World War II, President Franklin Roosevelt sidelined Vice President Henry Wallace in favor of Sen. Harry Truman of Missouri. Both of these new vice presidents succeeded to the presidency on the deaths of their war-time leaders only months after being inaugurated.

As this election approaches, President Bush needs a running mate who supports the war on terrorism as much as you do, but without your political liabilities. He also needs a running mate who might help unify the nation. Your Democratic opponent, Senator John Kerry, made overtures to Sen. John McCain to join him on a bipartisan "national unity" ticket of two war heroes.

If it was a good idea for Kerry, why would it not be an even better idea for Bush? Think of the broad political appeal of a Bush-McCain ticket, especially to political independents whose votes may decide the outcome. Yes, I know the relationship the president and the maverick Arizona senator is full of tension and rivalry, and McCain sometimes seems to go out of his way to aggravate the White House. But you could persuade President Bush that reaching out to his onetime rival (but strong supporter in the war on Iraq and terrorism) would be a magnanimous gesture — not unlike that of Ronald Reagan picking his former GOP rival, George H.W. Bush, as his running mate in 1980.

If not McCain, there are other intriguing running mate possibilities. Rudy Giuliani, who showed such great leadership as mayor of New York City after the terrorist attacks of 9/11, is an obvious one. Former Missouri senator John Danforth, a man of unquestioned integrity who presided with such grace at the funeral of Reagan, also comes to mind. If he's good enough to be the next U.S. ambassador to the United Nations, wouldn't he also be good enough to be vice president?

But you can draw up your own list of candidates. I hope that you will take it to President Bush and convince him that his chances of being re-elected — and maintaining the policies you've helped shape — are better with a new running mate. He will listen to you. You could even cast it in Reaganesque terms. Remind your boss that he is the heir to the Reagan political legacy and the keeper of the values that Reagan espoused. For those values to triumph in 2004, it may be necessary for you to take a hit for the team, so that President Bush can win one for the Gipper.

Sincerely,
James P. Gannon

Obviously, Cheney and Bush did not take my advice, and won anyway. But I still like the thought of Vice President McCain, in training for 2008.

POLITICIANS SHOULD STOP PANDERING TO SENIORS

USA Today, October 5, 2004

Last July I crossed that golden-age threshold into senior citizenship, receiving a Medicare card, a Medigap insurance policy from AARP and my new status as a member of America's most pampered class and most feared voter group.

Turning age 65 is like joining a club. There are special privileges, exclusive benefits, endless promises of good things to come, and a whole class of fawning, eager-to-please attendants who bow and scrape and ask what more they can do to make us comfortable and happy. This last group is known as politicians.

I have been watching presidential elections as a journalist for over 40 years, but this is my first election to watch as a senior citizen, and it just about makes me sick. At a time when America's young soldiers are dying in Iraq, America's young children are attending under-performing schools, and many young American families are struggling to make ends meet, our politicians act as if we older people are the neediest class and the highest priority of the government.

John Kerry and President Bush run from one campaign event to another, dueling verbally over who can promise the most to senior voters. Kerry expresses outrage at the Bush Administration's announcement last month of a 17.5% increase in Medicare insurance premiums for 2005. He says Bush "is driving our seniors right out of the middle class" and "socking seniors with the largest Medicare hike in history."

The Bush campaign retorts that Kerry opposed the new Medicare prescription drug benefit for seniors, and that the Massachusetts senator voted to require higher Medicare insurance premiums before he turned against them.

This campaign rhetoric overlooks the fact that senior citizens have been treated as America's most cared-for age group for the last three decades. We are gobbling up an ever-growing share of the federal budget, squeezing resources available to other needy groups that lack our political clout.

Since the passage of the Medicare health insurance program in 1965, the economic lot of the elderly has vastly improved. The same cannot be said for children. Fewer and fewer old people are poor, thanks much to Medicare, increases in Social Security and other programs for the aged. According to the U.S. Census Bureau, only 10.2% of Americans over age 65 had incomes below the official poverty line in 2003, down from 28.5% in 1966. But the poverty rate among children of all races was 17.6% in 2003, slightly more than it was in 1966. There are nearly four times as many poor children in the nation as there are poor seniors.

So why don't we see Bush and Kerry running from one day-care center to another promising more programs for kids? Because kids don't vote, and too often, neither do their low-income parents. And kids don't have a good lobbying force in Washington. We seniors do vote (two-thirds of us turned out in 2000) and we have the AARP and an army of briefcase-toting suits in Washington to argue our pressing needs. The fact that seniors dominate the key swing state of Florida, which both sides see as crucial to victory, only adds to our clout.

Last year, in a pre-emptive strike to win the senior vote in 2004, President Bush pushed Congress to pass the most massive increase in Medicare spending since Lyndon Johnson launched the program. This new prescription-drug benefit for seniors is projected to cost $564 billion over the next 10 years. Contrast this $56 billion annual handout to seniors with what the federal government spends on all veterans' benefits ($28.5 billion) or aid to low-income schools ($13.3 billion) or nutrition programs for poor single mothers with young kids ($4.8 billion), and you see how coddled we old folks really are.

The Democrats, who would have hailed this drug benefit as a progressive milestone had President Bill Clinton been able to pass it in his eight years, were appalled at the idea of Bush hijacking the Medicare issue, so they promptly set out to trash the program as cheap and inadequate. They managed to convince many seniors that they deserved much more, and polls show the drug benefit widely unpopular. Thus does the biggest handout to old folks since LBJ become as appealing as a $49 suit or a $2 bottle of wine.

I suppose I should be outraged, but to me, Medicare seems like a bargain. The $78.20 monthly premium my wife and I each will pay still leaves us with health insurance that costs less than half what I was paying under an employer-supported plan in effect until I turned 65. The $11.60 monthly increase is about enough for us to eat lunch at McDonalds, and guess how much we'll miss that?

All this should leave seniors thankful and appreciative, but politicians keep telling us that nothing is too good for us, and too many seniors act as if nothing will satisfy us. Frankly, I don't want to join the "greedy geezer" class. And I don't think most seniors are really so selfish that they want to steal resources from their children and grandchildren to protect themselves from paying any of the rising costs of growing old.

In this election, I am more concerned about those soldiers in Iraq, those kids in failing schools, and the threat that terrorists are going to strike our cities. The world that my six kids and ten grandkids are going to live in is way more important to me than the golden-age goodies promised by pandering politicians.

THE ECHO OF HISTORY: BUSH AND GRANT

USA Today, October 18, 2004

Ulysses S. Grant is widely remembered as a great general and a poor president. In his new biography of the 18th president, historian Josiah Bunting III notes that pundits and historians have tended to write of Grant the president with "condescension." Bunting sums up this view of Grant: "There may be strength in his soul, but no fineness in it, no grace; little culture, small learning ... meager evidence of the capacity to learn and reflect; no felt obligation to explain himself; no evidence of self-doubt."

If those words strike you as remarkably similar to the view of President Bush that is dominant in academia, much of the media and urban-oriented blue-state America, then you see one of the parallels between Grant and Bush that fairly leap off the pages of Bunting's fascinating book.

These similarities struck me with particular clarity during the recent round of debates between the president and his Democratic opponent, Sen. John Kerry, that polar opposite of Bush in ideology, culture and worldview.

It's worth pondering the parallels between Grant and Bush because the American people are about to decide what qualities they want in their president, and the choice has rarely been starker. Bush, for good or ill, shows many of the same character traits, strengths and weaknesses as the Union general who became known as "Unconditional Surrender" Grant — whose single-minded pursuit of victory at whatever the cost ultimately won the Civil War, but whose naive trust in and loyalty to his friends resulted in a scandal-marked presidency.

Grant was neither cultured nor eloquent. Bunting calls him a "stumpy, awkward, bashful man" of few words, who won a reputation in the Civil War as "a fighter not a talker." He was a rough-cut Westerner, a cigar-chewing general who would sit on a stump during battles, oblivious to personal danger, issuing terse orders.

As the casualties piled up and the Northern press called him a "butcher," he bulldozed ahead, never second-guessing himself through the blood-soaked horrors of 1864 to a final armistice at Appomattox, Va., in 1865. His tenacity, like Bush's regarding Iraq, was widely questioned during the war, but later cited as crucial to victory

As a general-turned-politician, Grant was a poor public speaker. He could write clear and precise battle orders but couldn't give a decent speech. Bunting believes that was no handicap to Grant as president. "America has always loved a tongue-tied hero, a Charles Lindbergh, a Lou Gehrig," Bunting writes. "Here was the very incarnation of Act not Talk."

That, too, is what millions of Americans admire in George W. Bush: He is Act, not Talk. The contrast between Bush and Kerry on this count is telling. The president clearly was outclassed on eloquence in the debates, where Kerry's mastery of language and argument was evident. But Bush's record as president shows a willingness to make big decisions, take big risks, stick with a course of action and play for victory. This is the essence of strong leadership.

The doubts about Kerry run to the opposite qualities: Is he too indecisive, too politically calculating and too quick to change positions under pressure — all too much Talk not Act?

This is Bunting's take on Grant's decisiveness: "Grant was willing to make decisions and live with their consequences, sustained, as William Tecumseh Sherman once said, by a constant faith in victory." Bush was willing to gamble his presidency on war with Iraq and seems sustained by an unshakable faith that freedom will triumph over terrorism. He will live with the consequences, which could arrive on Nov. 2.

Bunting uses Grant's first inaugural address of 1869 to make a point. The author calls that speech "the labored effort of a man trying his best to say what he believes" — which sounds like a description of Bush in the recent debates. But Americans trusted Grant and were reassured by his heartfelt words. "An honest, competent person laboring to communicate his convictions is far more persuasive than a fluent declaimer whose character the audience may have doubts about," Bunting writes.

Democrats contend that Bush is neither honest nor competent, just inarticulate. Republicans concede that Bush often labors to communicate his convictions but argue it's clear he has convictions, which shape and guide his decisions.

Kerry has raised doubts about his character and apparent lack of convictions by his habit of politically tacking left and right, as if windsurfing through the campaign, and his penchant for trying to have issues both ways. (He says he's morally against abortion but always votes to protect its legality; he says he opposes gay marriage but voted against the Defense of Marriage act; he voted to authorize war against Iraq but not Bush's method of war against Iraq, etc.)

President Grant was re-elected in a landslide in 1872, a feat Bush can hardly expect to match. But Grant's second term was disappointing, marked by scandals made worse by Grant's blind faith in his associates and reluctance to fire an incompetent friend or confront a venal ally. Democrats see parallels in Bush — think Halliburton and his unwavering support of Vice President Cheney and Defense Secretary Donald Rumsfeld, among others.

Whether Bush is re-elected may depend heavily on whether voters see him as Grant, the strong commander determined to win, or Grant, the weak administrator whose presidency was tarnished by incompetence and scandal.

9

IN MEMORIAM

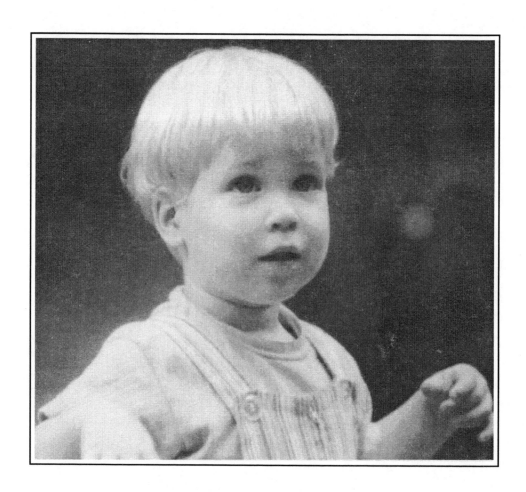

In Memoriam

There is one subject that I was never able to write about—the sudden death of our son, Patrick James Gannon, at the age of two years and nine months, in 1972. The following is the only piece in this book that never before has been published. I decided to include it here because this book, which is in many respects autobiographical, would seem incomplete without any reference to this pivotal event in my life, and the lives of all in the family. I wrote this letter to my parents ten days after Patrick died following a very brief illness.

September 25, 1972

Dear Mom and Dad,

It is difficult to know how to begin this letter about our beloved son Patrick, his life and his death. But I do want to share some thoughts with you about him, and what he meant to us, and how he changed our lives. I guess it is easiest to begin at the beginning.

Patrick's birth in January of 1970 in Pittsburgh was one of the most memorable experiences of my life. I was present with Joan in the delivery room and we shared the experience of his birth, which was an event of great emotional impact. I had never witnessed a birth before. It was a beautiful experience that brought Joan and me closer together. But it had a lasting effect on my relationship with Pat too; from that first breath of his, there was a special closeness that I have not felt with any other child, though I do love all my children deeply.

I felt a special bond with Patrick from that first moment all through his short life. I never cared much for babies, really. Until a child is about a year old, they seem to be more a nuisance than anything else. After that, of course, they develop their own personalities and become more fun to have around. But with Pat, I enjoyed his infancy from the first days on through his first year. I don't know why this was so, but it was.

Pat became very much a daddy's boy. He demanded much of my time and attention, and I gladly gave it. In the past year, he was virtually a constant companion whenever I was home. Pat and I spent a lot of time together alone. He loved to ride in my Fiat convertible, which he called "the little car." We had a special place in Sligo Creek Park, just five minutes from our home in Silver Spring, where Pat loved to go; his favorite pastime was to throw rocks in the creek and watch the splash. We went there often. I bought a small seat for the back of my bicycle, and Pat would ride with me around the neighborhood, objecting only when I would take him home. He would often take my hand and pull me out to the back yard, to play in the sand box, or push him on the tire swing which I'd hung on a big tree there.

Pat was always happy, always looking for some more fun, for something else to do — especially if Daddy would do it. Whenever we finished a ride or some play, he would ask, "What else?" There was always something else he wanted to do.

When I would come home from work at night, Pat would often be waiting at the front door, or would run down the street when he saw me coming from the bus stop, to greet me. When I was away for three weeks on my recent trip to Miami and California, he talked to me on the phone a few times, just as the other kids did. "Why you go, daddy? When you come home?" I can still hear the questions he asked, and it was always hard to explain why I wasn't at home.

I spent a lot of time with Pat after that trip, during my days off, not realizing of course that it was the twilight of his life. I cherish those hours now.

I spent Pat's last hours with him too. In the hospital, I stayed with him in the afternoon so that Joan could go home for a while and take care of the other children. We had thought that one of us probably would have to spend the night in the hospital with Pat, and Joan needed some rest, so she went home.

Just as I was there in the beginning, when Pat was born, so I was with him at the end, when he died. It is symbolic of the unique relationship that we had. Patrick provided me with what have been the most profound emotional experiences of my life — joy at his birth, and shock and pain at his death. In between, there was a memorable interlude of unforgettable joy. That has left a mark on me. Pat was just a little boy, but he has taught me so much about living to enjoy each moment of life, and loving without reserve.

What are we to make of this tragedy?

On a purely human level, it makes no sense. In natural terms, it seems a cruel, unbelievable blow, totally unexplainable. I refuse to think of it in those terms. To do so would be to rob the meaning of Pat's life, and wipe out the happiness he brought and replace it with bitterness and grief.

The only way that Pat's death becomes acceptable is on supernatural terms. Joan and I have thought much about this in the past few days, and I think we have come to terms with the reality on this level.

At Pat's funeral, I delivered a short eulogy trying to explain to our friends and relatives how Joan and I understand what has happened. I felt it was important for them to know how we view Pat's life and death and what meaning we find in it. I want you to know, too.

This is what I said from the pulpit at the funeral:

Patrick lived barely one thousand days, but those one thousand days were a time of joy and love and happiness like no other time we have known in our lives. We believe that Patrick had a mission in life, a mission from God: to teach us how to love one another better, and how to make the very best of the precious gift of life. Patrick accomplished that mission beautifully and when it was done, he returned to God.

Patrick never knew sin, or hate, or fear or pain. His life was one of happiness, joy and love, and I cannot think of a better kind of life. So please do not share the pain and grief we feel in Pat's death, but rather share the happiness and joy we knew in his beautiful life.

Above all, this we believe: that Patrick LIVES — and we will live with him again.

That's what I said in church. I want to add only one thought especially for you, mom and dad: that is to thank you for fostering in me the faith in the goodness of the Lord. Without the gift of faith, this cross would be unbearable. Pat is gone for now, but never will be forgotten. I believe that he changed our lives — all for the better. That was his reason for living.

Your loving son, Jim

Quick Order Form

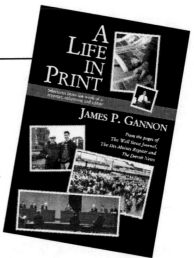

For additional copies of A Life in Print
by James P. Gannon
Perfect for:

- Gifts for friends or family members
- High school or college students interested in journalism and media careers
- Teachers of journalism, media or writing classes.

Order by phone: call 540/987-9536
On the web: www.blackwaterpublications.com
Order by e-mail to: blackwaterpub@earthlink.net
Order by Mail: fill out form below

Name _____

Address_____

City _____ State _____ Zip _____

Enclose $14.95 for each copy, plus $4 for shipping one book, or $5 for two books. Virginia residents add 5% sales tax ($0.75) or $15.70 per book, plus shipping.
Make check to Blackwater Publications.
Mail to: Blackwater Publications, P.O. Box 80, Boston, VA 22713

If you want an author-signed copy, check here_____

Money-back guarantee: Returnable for a full refund if you are unsatisfied for any reason.

Blackwater Publications offers these other fine books:

BEYOND THE RIM: FROM SLAVERY TO REDEMPTION IN RAPPAHANNOCK COUNTY, VIRGINIA
By James D. Russell
Soft cover, 110 pages, illustrated, $14.95
ISBN: 0976452812

Beyond the Rim is a unique work of black folk history, telling the true story of "Sistah Cahline" Terry, who toiled as a slave on plantations in Rappahannock and Culpeper Counties in Virginia. She saw the Civil War, bore the children of a white slave-master, and endured to live to the age of 108. It is a stirring tale told with humor and insight by her 84-year-old great-grandson, who as a child heard these stories of slavery days from an independent, feisty woman who never gave up her thirst for freedom and dignity.

IRISH REBELS, CONFEDERATE TIGERS: A HISTORY OF THE 6TH LOUISIANA VOLUNTEERS, 1861-1865
By James P. Gannon
Hard cover, 454 pages, illustrated with maps and photos, $29.00
ISBN: 1882810163

This history of the long-forgotten Irish soldiers of the Confederate Army traces the origins and bloody history of this fighting regiment composed mostly of Irish immigrants who settled in New Orleans before the Civil War. They battled their way from First Manassas to the surrender at Appomattox as part of Gen. Robert E. Lee's army, a colorful brotherhood of fighters, rowdy in camp and fierce on the battlefield. This gripping narrative is supplemented with a complete roster of the 1,200 men of the 6th Louisiana, giving dates and details of each man's service.

Irish Rebels, Confederate Tigers "is a poignant, serious and entertaining military history about a gritty, tenacious, largely Irish regiment from New Orleans that fought in almost every major battle in the War Between the States...Gannon's intense and thorough research is impressive."
Columnist Angus Lind in The Times-Picayune, New Orleans
"... A first-rate regimental history....Gannon writes a smoothly flowing narrative... You get to know the men and care what happens to them. The battle narrations are clear and concise, supplemented with a lot of first-rate maps."
The Civil War News

Order on-line at www.blackwaterpublications.com. Or send check to: Blackwater Publications, P.O. Box 80, Boston, VA 22713. Add $4 for shipping. Virginia residents add 5% sales tax. E-mail orders may be sent to blackwaterpub@earthlink.net.